Following the Good Shepherd

Psalm 23

by
Danny Bond

Word Transfer Publishers
Laguna Hills, California

Following The Good Shepherd

Psalm 23

All scripture is taken from The Holy Bible,
New King James version, unless otherwise
noted.

First printing, October 1990
ISBN # 1-877654-03-5
Copyright 1990 by Danny Bond.
All rights reserved.
Printed in the United States of America.

To my three children,
Laurie Beth, Daniel, and Diana
for all the laughter, joy, and love
you have brought into my life.
May this book help you come to know
in an intimately satisfying and saving way,
the God of your father.

Table of Contents

I Shall Not Want

Psalm 23:1

**THE LORD is
my shepherd;
I shall not want.**

1

The words we are about to study are those of a man who truly knew God. In an effort to describe the richness of his experience as a man after God's own heart, David chose to draw upon his youthful experience as a shepherd. In his analogy he describes the detailed provision, protection, and hope of a man who *sincerely follows after his God.* The result is this timeless piece of encouragement for all believers. David writes:

The Lord is my shepherd;
I shall not want.
He makes me to lie down in green pastures;
He leads me beside the still waters.
He restores my soul;
He leads me in the paths of righteousness
For His name's sake.
Yea, though I walk through the valley of the
shadow of death,
I will fear no evil;
For You are with me;
Your rod and Your staff, they comfort me.
You prepare a table before me in the presence of my enemies;
You anoint my head with oil;
My cup runs over.
Surely goodness and mercy shall follow me
All the days of my life;
And I will dwell in the house of the Lord
Forever.   (Psalm 23)

THE LORD

What does it mean to have the Lord as your Shepherd? David says that *the Lord* is his Shepherd. The word translated "shepherd" is the Hebrew word *Ra'ah* and it means, literally, "to tend a flock," "to make friendship with," or "to keep company with." David is saying that he knew the deep blessings of being guided and taken care of by God. His message to us is how God, his main source of guidance and provision, is also his closest Friend with whom he loves to spend his time. The rest of this Psalm lists, in colorful detail, all of the benefits of having the Lord as our Shepherd.

How is this important to us today? We live in such a complex, fast-paced society that we are easily susceptible to allowing many different things to "shepherd" us. Yet the beauty of this Psalm shows us that what was true for David, in a much simpler and slower-paced society, still holds just as true for us today. For the Lord tells us in His Word, "I am the Lord; I change not." It becomes quickly evident upon reading the life of David why he was such a phenomenal person: he had only one source of guidance—the Lord Himself.

Other Shepherds

It is God's desire for this to be the case in all of our lives. However, we often allow other things to take His place. You might allow your pastor or psychologist to be your shepherd instead of Jesus. Some people go beyond that and find their lives becoming controlled by their jobs. As the old saying goes, "I sold my soul to the company store." Their lives are completely run by the dictates of their employers. People allow all kinds of things (career, school, goals in life, job, and even TV) to

14

ultimately shepherd them. Television is one of the greatest sources of distraction to the Christian today. You may want to stop right here for a moment and ask yourself if any of these things has usurped the Lord's place in your life.

Jesus is the Good Shepherd

Jesus Christ taught that He Himself is the Good Shepherd David spoke of. In John 10:11, He says, "I am the good shepherd. The good shepherd gives His life for the sheep."

Because the *Lord* was David's Shepherd, he did not lack anything he needed. As simple as this statement may seem, the idea of God being our Shepherd carries with it an entire world of security that is often missed in a casual reading of this Psalm.

One great preacher of the last century put it this way: "He is the good shepherd, because all that ought to be done, all that can be done, all that he may wish to be done towards his sheep he does! Never did a shepherd so intensely throw his soul into his calling as The Good Shepherd. His power is their defense. He lifts up his hand and says, 'I give to my sheep eternal life, and they shall never perish, neither shall any man pluck them out of my hand.' His wisdom is their guidance, his love is their perpetual shield, his infinity is their storehouse, and his omniscience is their protection." You cannot find better care, guidance, and friendship than from the Living God Himself!

MY SHEPHERD

Notice that he says, "The Lord is *my* shepherd." David realized that his life belonged to the Lord; God was his personal Shepherd. Jesus says, "I am the good shepherd; and I know My sheep, and am known by My own."(John 10:14). Before we go any further, it is important that you ask yourself this question: "Do I, like David, belong to the Good Shepherd?" This is crucial because until you receive Him as your Lord and Savior, He cannot be your Shepherd. You might say, "Can't God be my guide and friend without Jesus?" Let's let Jesus answer that question Himself.

In the Lord's teaching, He made it clear that He is the only way to God. "Jesus said to him, 'I am the way, the truth, and the life. No one comes to the Father except through me' " (John 14:6). In another place He spoke of this relationship in the same terms as David in Psalm 23: "Then Jesus said to them again, 'Most assuredly, I say to you, I am the door of the sheep' " (John 10:7).

The Door

Several friends were traveling in Palestine. They reached a high ridge overlooking the village of Bethlehem. Seeing a sheepfold, they went in. In a few moments the owner appeared, a veteran shepherd. "Is this your sheepfold?" asked one of the travelers. "Aye," was the quick reply. "And is this where the sheep sleep?" pointing to a rough shelter thrown up against the rock in a corner. The shepherd nodded.

"But there is no gate to the fold; how do you close the sheep in at night?" The old shepherd looked at the two travelers as though they should have known better.

"I am the door," he said assuringly; and gathering his loose robe tightly around his ankles, he was down in a moment, squatting in the doorway, his back against one post, his feet against the other, his knees drawn up and clasped by his weather-beaten hands. Gently he bowed his head and closed his eyes, as

16

many a time he had closed them to catch a few hours' sleep under the starlight.

"I am the door," he repeated again and again. "I watch the sheep throughout the night." Then he added with a note of triumph in his voice, "And I have never lost a lamb from my fold yet."

When we trust in Him as Savior, He becomes our Shepherd. He is not everybody's Shepherd. Many people assume He has become their Shepherd because they are now attending a church. He is only your Shepherd if you have come through the door into the fold of His sheep. The Lord Jesus said in John 10:9, "I am the door. If anyone enters by Me, he will be saved, and will go in and out and find pasture." The way to receive Him is to bow before Him as your Lord, confessing your desire to turn from your sin and walk with Him in a personal relationship. Ask Him to come and live in your heart right now.

Do I Belong to Him?

How do we know if we belong to the Good Shepherd? How do we know if we need to make that step? We have to ask ourselves a very crucial question: "Have I heard His voice?" Jesus says, "I am the Good Shepherd... My sheep hear my voice." Can you say, "The Lord is my Shepherd; I shall not want"? You can if you know His voice. (We will examine in detail how we actually hear the voice of God in a later chapter. For now, however, we will keep this issue very simple.) If you know the voice of Jesus, then He is your Shepherd. We see an excellent example of this in the conversion of Paul the apostle.

Following His Voice

Paul the apostle was on the Damascus Road when he was converted. The first thing that happened after

17

his conversion was that he heard the voice of Jesus Christ. Paul asked Jesus, "Who are you, Lord?" and the Lord began to speak to him. From that point until he went through the valley of the shadow of death, Paul heard and followed the voice of the Lord. That is effectively the picture David paints for us in this Psalm: A sheep following the Good Shepherd all through this life and ultimately into heaven. One of the ways we know that we belong to the Good Shepherd is that *we hear His voice and follow Him.* In John 10:27, Jesus says, "My sheep hear My voice, and I know them, and they follow Me." Everything David talks about in this Psalm and that we will discuss in this book revolves around this one basic issue. If we will not follow, we cannot experience the green pastures, the still waters, or any of the other blessings outlined here. There is a good reason for this. It has to do with something we have very much in common with sheep.

No Sense of Direction

An interesting thing about sheep is that they lack all sense of direction. If you turn a sheep loose in the front yard of your house, unlike your dog, he will not come back. You will never see him again; he'll just wander and wander. Though sheep have absolutely no sense of direction, God has blessed them with one great quality, *they have very good ears.*

A good illustration of this point is about a man who was traveling in Syria and came to a place where three different shepherds were watering their sheep, all crowded around the same well. The traveler was wondering how they were going to separate the sheep. As he watched, he found his answer. Soon one shepherd raised his hands to his mouth and called, "Men-ah!" the Arabic for "Follow me"; and immediately thirty sheep clambered up

the hill after him. Not one of his sheep remained.
Each had responded immediately to their shepherd's
voice. It is as Jesus says, "My sheep hear My voice...
and they follow Me."

New Ears

One of the greatest blessings of being under
the care of the Good Shepherd is that we receive
a brand new set of sheep's ears. These are actually
spiritual ears. With these new ears we are able to
hear the voice of God for the first time. It is good
that we get a new set of ears because the Bible
says, ."O Lord, I know the way of man is not in
himself..." (Jeremiah 10:23). Man, just like a
sheep, has a very bad sense of direction. If you leave
a man unto himself, he will wander aimlessly
through life.

The Lord has given believers new ears because we
do not know how to guide our own lives. God has
created us with unique talents, gifts, and insights,
but we do not have the ability within ourselves to
properly manage these abilities.

For example, many people make the decision
in high school to go to college to pursue a particular
profession. By the time they finish college they
have changed their minds, and in many cases it's
too late. Facing the crisis of the moment, which
is the need to support themselves, they are forced
to get the job they have been training for all
those years. Consequently, they live the rest of
their lives in frustration because of an earlier
incapacity to make the proper choice. All of that
is to say: Man does not know the way to his
own happiness.

This holds true in the spiritual realm. The way
of God does not lie within us. We will never know
fulfillment in the rich, satisfying life God has
ordained for us until we get our ears fixed and

19

begin to follow the Good Shepherd's voice.

If you are still marching through life in your own direction, to the beat of your own drum, then you are marching into emptiness. You have a very bad sense of direction on your own.

The Lord says, "I will instruct you and teach you in the way you should go; I will guide you with My eye" (Psalm 32:8). Notice that the Lord promises He will instruct us. This truth is getting lost in present-day Christianity. Too often these days, that intensely personal relationship with Jesus is substituted with all the programs religious man in his "wisdom" has invented to replace the work and guidance of the Holy Spirit.

The way to go does not lie within us. We cannot see what is ahead for the next day, week, or year. But God does.

In Isaiah 30:21 God says, "Your ears shall hear..." God wants to speak into our spiritual ears and tell us the way to walk.

Back to the Question

Let's go back to our original question. How can I know if the Lord Jesus Christ is my personal Shepherd? The Bible teaches that we know the Lord is our Shepherd because we have heard His voice. Whether you are today a sheep who is following closely or one who is following far off, if you have come to know the Good Shepherd, then to some degree you know His voice *speaking to your heart.*

People have often said to me that they never hear the voice of God. I certainly would not be alarmed if you do not hear His voice audibly. (We will discuss this in a later chapter). However, if you do not hear His voice by the impressions He places on your heart, then something is wrong, because Jesus clearly says, "My sheep know My voice."

20

His Alone

If the Lord is your Shepherd, then you should be able to say with gladness, "I belong to the Lord. Everything that I am is His, and He is mine."

To this day, when a shepherd owns a flock of sheep, they are his to do with as he pleases. If he wishes to take one sheep, feed him well, have his wool grow long, and then shear the wool to make a sweater, that is his prerogative. He is the shepherd; he owns the sheep. If he would like to take another sheep, make him a pet, and lead him around on a little leash, it is allowed. If David, being a shepherd, wanted to take one of the sheep and offer him as a sacrifice to the Lord, he could do that.

If the Lord is your Shepherd, then you should be able to say without hesitation, "My life belongs to Him, He can do with me whatever He pleases." Often we fall into the trap of wanting the blessings the Lord desires to bestow upon us, but not wanting to follow Him as our Shepherd. We find an example of this in the Old Testament.

Benefits and Responsibility

Balaam, an Old Testament prophet, wanted to die the death of the righteous. He wanted all the benefits of being under the care of God, but the Bible tells us he loved the wages of unrighteousness. Therefore he perished without God into everlasting destruction. Often, people will want the care of the Good Shepherd, but fail to follow what He says. They do not want to assume the responsibility.

The apostle Paul realized this when he said in 2 Corinthians 12:15, "...I will very gladly spend and be spent for your souls..." There Paul revealed that behind all of his service was the fact that he had already given his life completely to God; hence, he was free to expand His kingdom.

21

There is a seal that was used by the old American Missionary Society which had the picture of an ox standing between an altar and a plow. The motto underneath said, "Ready for Either." That reminds me of a period in Christianity when people were ready at any time to give their lives to the Lord as an offering or in service. May God help us to return to that kind of commitment to Him.

All of this is bound up in the fact that David knew the Lord was *his* Shepherd. When we come to the place where we share David's commitment to the Lord, we are able to say along with him, in honesty and confidence, "I shall not want." It is then that we shall know true contentment.

I SHALL NOT WANT

Many Christians are looking for some great experience to take place in their lives that will bring them to the place where they will finally become content. Some see this as the day when they will finally have that particular ministry for which they have been longing. Others see it as when they are married. Yet God loves us so much, He would like to make us content right now. David was content because he knew the Lord was his Shepherd. What a wonderful thing it is to have our hearts filled with contentment because we know the Lord and are under His daily care. After many years of walking with the Lord, Paul summed up his experience by saying, "But godliness with contentment is great gain" (1 Timothy 6:6).

David is speaking of what Jesus later called "the abundant life." Jesus says, "I have come that they may have life, and that they may have it more abundantly" (John 10:10). We will never lack anything necessary as long as the Lord is our Shepherd.

You might ask, "How long is He going to be my Shepherd?" The Lord will be our Shepherd as long as He lives. The writer to the Hebrews says, "Jesus Christ is the same yesterday, today, and forever" (Hebrews 13:8). He is going to take care of us and eternally meet our needs.

God Determines Our Need

Yet it is God, not us, who determines what we need and what we do not need. If it were up to us, we would never be satisfied.

Occasionally, the Lord determines it is to our benefit to be humbled. For example, there may be some lean times as the Good Shepherd is disciplining us to show us that we can trust in Him. Some of the best times in my life have been in the lean times. There have been those seasons when there did not seem to be enough money, care, and provision; yet somehow we made it. There was a time when the rent was due and they put the slip on our front door that said, "You must pay or move out in three days." I remember coming home and seeing that notice and wondering what the Lord had in mind. Somebody once had said, "God's always on time; He is never too late." But I thought, "This is it! They are going to throw us out on the street." Well, they didn't— because *the Lord is faithful.* He will determine what our needs are and then He will meet those needs in His time. One thing we often overlook in this process is that it is God's desire at all times to bring about an increase in our faith. I thank God for the times He stretches us in our faith to the point where we find ourselves intensely turning the pages of our Bibles, looking for another promise to keep us going.

Stretching Our Faith

The New Testament gives an account of Jesus walking on water and Simon Peter wanting to join him. Though Peter got out of the boat and began to walk to Jesus, there were other men who remained. Why did he step out? Peter got out of the boat because he wanted to be where Jesus was. The Lord sustained him as far as his faith would carry him; then he began to sink. That's the way our faith grows. God takes us to the very end of our faith and then lets us start sinking before He pulls us out again.

We need to understand that when the Lord allows us those times when we seem to be wanting, it's usually to build our faith. He pulls us out and then our faith is strengthened. Hence, the next time we can walk a little farther on the water; and the routine of building our faith goes on.

In Romans 8:32, Paul writes, "He who did not spare His own Son, but delivered Him up for us all, how shall He not with Him also freely give us all things?"

Psalm 34:10 says, "The young lions lack and suffer hunger; but those who seek the Lord shall not lack any good thing." That is an absolute promise.

In Philippians 4:19, Paul writes, "And my God shall supply all your needs..." It says *all* your needs. That means spiritual and physical, "...according to His riches in glory by Christ Jesus."

At this point you might be wondering, "Is there anything *I* can do to further my experience of seeing the Lord provide all of my needs?"

Involvement and Provision

There is no better way to see the Lord's provision in our lives than to get involved in what He is doing. When we start to get involved in God's work, we begin to see that provision in our lives in a much more specific way.

We see a classic example of this wonderful truth in the Old Testament account of Elijah the prophet and the widow: "Then the word of the Lord came to him, saying, 'Arise, go to Zarephath, which belongs to Sidon, and dwell there. See, I have commanded a widow there to provide for you.' So he arose and went to Zarephath. And when he came to the gate of the city, indeed a widow was there gathering sticks. And he called to her and said, 'Please bring me a little water in a cup, that I may drink.' And as she was going to get it, he called to her and said, 'Please bring me a morsel of bread in your hand.'

"Then she said, 'As the Lord your God lives, I do not have bread, only a handful of flour in a bin, and a little oil in a jar; and see, I am gathering a couple of sticks that I may go in and prepare it for myself and my son, that we may eat it, and die.'

"And Elijah said to her, 'Do not fear; go and do as you have said, but make me a small cake from it first, and bring it to me; and afterward make some for yourself and your son. For thus says the Lord God of Israel: "The bin of flour shall not be used up, nor shall the jar of oil run dry, until the day the Lord sends rain on the earth."'

"So she went away and did according to the word of Elijah; and she and he and her household ate for many days. The bin of flour was not used up, nor did the jar of oil run dry, according to the word of the Lord which He spoke by Elijah" (1 Kings 17:8-16).

Here is a woman who has run out of everything and realizes she is about to die. At the point when it seems she has the least to offer, God calls her to get involved in His work. As she gets involved in the Lord's work and obeys the voice of God through the prophet Elijah, the provision of the Lord miraculously comes to her over and over again.

Can you imagine going every day with just enough flour and oil to bake one cake? You make that and come back and there's just enough left to make another meal. Then you take that, use it, go back, and again there's just enough. We see examples of the same type of provision throughout the Bible.

When men and women of God give themselves to His work, they enter into the kind of provision where they can step back and say, "The Lord is my Shepherd; I shall not want."

What a lesson there is to be learned here. Step out, and let God begin to use you. Step out, as the Holy Spirit leads you to where you see a need, and watch the Lord begin to do the miraculous as He did with this widow.

In Luke 6:38, Jesus says, "Give, and it will be given to you: good measure, pressed down, shaken together, and running over will be put into your bosom. For with the same measure that you use, it will be measured back to you." As we let go, giving our lives over to His work, with the same scoop we are using to give out, God is going to pour His blessings right back into our lives.

Benefits of Staying Close

If you will study a shepherd working closely with his sheep, you will discover that it is the sheep that stay the closest to the shepherd who receive the best that the shepherd has to offer.

In the East, there often springs up an intimate affection between the shepherd and his sheep. There are some sheep that will always keep at a distance from the shepherd; if he sits down at one end of a field, they are pretty sure to be at the other end. But there are others that keep closer to him, and there are some that are so fond of the shepherd that you never see him without also seeing them close by his side. If he stops, they stop; if he moves, they move. They love the pasture, but they love the shepherd better still.

The interesting thing is that these sheep are generally the fattest of the flock because the shepherd is sure to give them the best of food. They love him and he loves them; he loves all the sheep, but he loves these with a very special kind of love. Thus, the believers who abide closest to our Lord enjoy the highest level of true happiness and the deepest experience of real spiritual enjoyment.

When we draw close to the Lord and step out into His work, we make ourselves one of those who is going to stick much closer to the Lord than the sheep out there on the edge. It is then that we know the marvelous blessing of hearing His voice with those new sheep's ears, which fills our hearts with confidence that we belong to Him. And it is then that we experience the joy of coming under the care of the Good Shepherd, and being fed by His hand. I believe it is the birthright of every child of God to be able to live so near to Him that we have the confidence He will meet our every need.

One Sunday morning a long time ago, a little girl summed up what we have seen so far. She was called upon to quote the first verse of the Twenty-third Psalm. She stood up and said, "The Lord is my shepherd; *that's all I want.*"

The Way into
Peace
and Rest

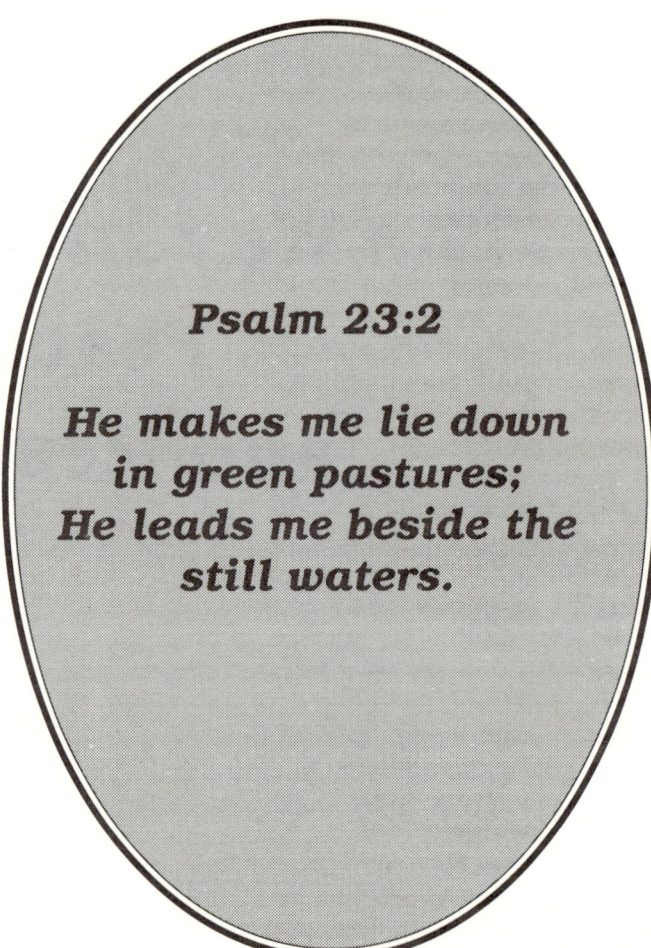

Psalm 23:2

He makes me lie down in green pastures; He leads me beside the still waters.

2

I once read that eight percent of what people worry about is actually legitimate and the other ninety-two percent is either something future over which we have no control, or it's something that is not even realistic that we are fabricating in our minds. There are so many things in life that distract and rob us of the peace that God has freely made available to us. In this chapter we will examine some of these issues and how to overcome them. Then we can go on to say with David, "He makes me to lie down in green pastures; He leads me beside the still waters."

We have in our text a picture of the contentment and peace which comes as a result of being under the care and guidance of the Good Shepherd.

The Nature of Sheep

To begin with, we need to realize that sheep do not naturally lie down and rest in peace on their own. It takes a lot of work and care on the part of the shepherd to enable them to do so. It is amazing to see the parallel needs in our own lives. It becomes obvious why God so often likens His people to the sheep of His pasture. There are so many things in life that rob us of our peace that it takes a tremendous amount of the Lord's work in our lives to bring us into His rest.

Concerning sheep, there are basically four issues involved in getting them to lie down in green pastures: First, sheep must have their fears dealt with.

Second, they must be free from friction with those around them. Third, they must be well fed. Fourth, if a sheep is to have the contentment and the rest that the shepherd would like to give him, he *must* follow his shepherd. In this chapter we will examine these four issues and see how they apply to us as we seek to follow Jesus as our Good Shepherd.

FEAR

David says, "He makes me to lie down." This phrase expresses the shepherd's involvement in bringing them to this place. By nature, sheep are very fearful and nervous creatures. Aside from the protection of their shepherd, they are completely unable to deal with their enemies and afflictions in life. They have no method of defense. Just about every other animal has some means of defense. A dog, for instance, may not be very big; but, when he opens his mouth, you can see that he has some very sharp teeth inside, and he can bite pretty hard. That is his means of defense. Though most of the animal kingdom has some means of defense, the sheep does not; he does not have sharp teeth, he does not have any claws—he is altogether defenseless. His defense must come from the protection of the shepherd; as a result, there are many fears in the life of a sheep, especially if he gets away from the shepherd.

Our Fears

We are much like that; we have many fears by nature. The afflictions and enemies we face in the Christian life are very real; hence, each one of us wrestles with our own private fears. One person reading this book is probably worrying about where his money will come from to pay the rent this month, while another might be afraid they will never overcome a certain sin in their life. Still another is under the attack of Satan, wondering if they will still be standing when their current battle is over.

Timothy's Fear

All of us struggle with different fears. It is interesting that Timothy, Paul the apostle's number-one disciple, had a problem with fear. This was even after Paul had discipled him to such a degree that he said, "I've got no man like Timothy in my life." Though Timothy, the pastor of the church at Ephesus, was well taught in the things of God, he was still fearful. There were people teaching false doctrine in the church and there were people despising him because of his youth. Paul wrote to him about the issue of fear, saying, "For God has not given us a spirit of fear, but of power and of love and of a sound mind" (2 Timothy 1:7). The sound mind speaks of the idea of a mind that is free from fear, the kind that is solidly fixed on the care of God. Paul reminds Timothy that he is following the One who can take care of our problems. If we look to God, we will enter into the peace that He has for us. This understanding is the beginning of being led to the still waters.

David says, "He makes me to lie down in green pastures; He leads me beside the still waters." I think it helps us to remember that those words were penned by a man whose very life had been threatened on numerous occasions. He was a man with great experience in being filled with fear because of his enemies. But, more importantly, David had also experienced being delivered from that fear by the hand of God.

David's Secret

What was his secret? How was he able to say with such confidence, "He makes me to lie down in green pastures; He leads me beside the still waters"? The answer can be summed up in one word: prayer. The book of Psalms is the largest book in the Bible and so many of the chapters written by David revolve around prayer. This man, rejoicing over the peace and rest of our Good Shepherd, is first and foremost a true man of prayer.

How much peace do you have in your life? I am convinced that our peace/fear level is, in a very real sense, related to how much time we spend in prayer. Another example of this can be found in the life of the prophet Daniel.

Daniel's Example

The prophet Daniel lived at a time when the king decreed that nobody could pray to any other god except himself and his image. Daniel responded, in Daniel 6:10, by going in, shutting the door, and doing what he always did. Three times a day, he got down on his knees and came to the Lord in prayer. Because of his violation of the king's command, Daniel was captured and thrown into the lions' den. Most people would be terrified in this position, but the Bible testifies that Daniel was in perfect peace. We don't find a kicking, screaming, fighting Daniel being dragged toward the lions' den; he calmly went with them.

How could he respond so peacefully in the face of such affliction? It was because of prayer. This was a key issue in Daniel's life. How do we get to the place where we overcome the fears in our lives that we might lie down in green pastures, having the peace of God in our hearts? The Psalms of David and the example of Daniel show us the way: through prayer.

Requests Made Known

Another man with the ability to overcome fear and rest in the Lord was the apostle Paul. His life was filled with afflictions, uncertainties, and con-

34

stant danger. In the midst of it all, we find that he was one of the greatest men of prayer that the world has ever known. Every time he wrote a letter, he informed his readers that he was praying for them. I have discovered that if I want to learn more about the power of prayer, I need to follow the example of the men who walked in it.

Philippians 4:6 in the Amplified Bible says, "Do not fret or have any anxiety about anything, but in every circumstance and in everything, by prayer and petition (definite requests), with thanksgiving, continue to make your wants known to God." And then he goes on to tell us what will happen if we do that. Paul says, "And God's peace [shall be yours, that tranquil state of a soul assured of its salvation through Christ, and so fearing nothing from God and being content with its earthly lot of whatever sort that is, that peace] which transcends all understanding shall garrison and mount guard over your hearts and minds in Christ Jesus" (Philippians 4:7). Through prayer and supplication we can experience the Lord's peace as a garrison mounting guard around our hearts.

I have found that the best way to do this is simply to sit down before the Lord and earnestly discuss the things that are going on in my life. As I leave my burdens with Him, trusting Him for the results, the Lord is always faithful to meet my every need. I am convinced that we often continue in our fears and anxieties because we fail to take advantage of the great blessing of prayer.

Many of us are like the man who met a pastor while riding on the subway one day in New York City. While riding along, a middle-aged man sat down beside the pastor and opened a conversation. He unburdened his problems, telling the him how he had been to many places in New York, searching in vain for employment. He lamented the fact that he must face his wife again without a job. The kind pastor listened attentively to his long tale of woe until he finished and then asked, "Have you ever tried prayer?" "Oh no!" he replied, "Things haven't gotten that bad yet."

That is often the way we look at prayer. However, the Bible encourages us to pray at all times, not just for emergencies. God's promises are true. His Word says in 2 Corinthians 1:20, "For all the promises of God in Him are Yes, and in Him Amen, to the glory of God through us." We can trust Him.

Trusting Him

In contrast to the man on the subway, Chuck Smith tells how he was brought to a place of peace through prayer in the early days when Calvary Chapel of Costa Mesa, California, began to grow. By 1971, they had outgrown the small church and had begun seating the overflow of people on the patio. He writes: "By 1971, however, the large crowds and the winter rains forced us to move again. We bought a ten-acre tract of land on the Costa Mesa/Santa Ana border.... Soon after buying the land, we again did the unpredictable and erected a giant circus tent that could seat 1,600 at a stretch. This was soon enlarged to hold 2,000 seats. Meanwhile we began building an enormous sanctuary adjacent to it.

"This was all amazing to me—and a bit frightening. I would sit at the signal across the street looking at the bare lot that we had obligated ourselves to purchase, and start to panic. It would take a tremendous amount of money to develop the property. Was I being foolish to obligate these people to that kind of a project? Why not be satisfied where you are? I would think. The bills are all paid. You've got money in the bank. This is going to take such a great outlay. But then, one time as I sat there, the Lord spoke to my heart:

Whose church is it? I replied out loud, 'It's Your church, Lord.' *Then why are you worried about bankruptcy?*

"It was a relief. A sense of frantic worry just rolled off me. The finances were not my responsibility. They were His. This was an extremely important lesson for me to learn. It's not my church. It's His church" (Chuck Smith and Tal Brooke, *Harvest*, Old Tappan, N. J.: Chosen Books, 1987, pp. 24-25).

This incident illustrates everything we have been discussing. Here is a great man of God, a man of God's Word, a tremendous man of prayer, and he too has problems with fear. Yet what does his story tell us? As he sat before the Lord, the Lord saw his need and his anxiety and He replaced it with the perfect peace that passes all understanding.

As Paul explained to Timothy, God has not given us the spirit of fear, but of a sound mind. The way we enter into it is through bringing our fears to the Lord in prayer, as Peter tells us, "casting all your care upon Him, for He cares for you" (1 Peter 5:7).

FRICTION

A second thing about sheep is that they cannot rest beside the still waters unless they are free from friction with others. Though they are very cute-looking and defenseless, they can be mean at times. Though they have no sharp teeth, horns, or claws, they do have *very hard heads.*

Sheep have what is called a "butting order." This is brought about by one sheep wanting to exalt himself above all the others. One sheep will think he is to be the leader in the flock, so he will come up and begin to butt all of the other sheep around him until he has butted his way into preeminence. All of this can cause a tremendous amount of anxiety in the rest of the flock. At this point it is almost impossible to get them to lie down in peace.

Our Pride

I see such a parallel in this with our humanity. We are God's sheep, the sheep of His pasture; and in the Lord's church one of the greatest problems that we have is this same issue of self-exaltation. The Bible has a very concise word for this: *pride.* There is something inside of us that longs for the preeminence. It might be in our home, marriage, neighborhood, or work. We see it on the school campus: somebody wants to be the preeminent one in their peer group, to be "Number One." It occurs in the church, in various ministries, with friends and neighbors. Many bad decisions are made in our lives because of pride. The whole thing of wanting to have preeminence takes away the peace in our lives and replaces it with friction and anxiety.

In the last Epistle of the apostle John we read, "I wrote to the church, but Diotrephes, who loves to have the preeminence among them, does not receive us" (3 John 9). He is writing about a man who was causing a great disturbance in the church because of his lust for power. The Book of Proverbs warns, "By pride comes only contention..." (Proverbs 13:10). This problem is obviously *not* isolated to a church setting. Each one of us can look into the past and see far too many painful memories of times when we lost our peace because of pride.

The Example of Jesus

Have you ever noticed how pride crept into the Last Supper and stole the peace from that touching scene? On the night before our Lord's crucifixion, we find Jesus with a very heavy heart, explaining to the disciples that He is going to die. In the midst of this heart-rending situation, they are arguing among themselves about who is to be the greatest in the kingdom of heaven! Luke 22:24 says, "But there was

38

also rivalry among them, as to which of them should be considered the greatest." Can you imagine how it broke His heart? How did He deal with this astonishing display of pride? The Bible tells us that He "rose from supper and laid aside His garments, took a towel and girded Himself. After that, He poured water into a basin and began to wash the disciples' feet, and to wipe them with the towel with which He was girded" (John 13:4-5). By example, He showed them the solution to their problem. After giving them a graphic display of self-sacrificing humility, He called them to submit to that example.

"So when He had washed their feet, taken His garments, and sat down again, He said to them, 'Do you know what I have done to you? You call Me Teacher and Lord, and you say well, for so I am. If I then, your Lord and Teacher, have washed your feet, you also ought to wash one another's feet'" (John 13:12-14).

Pride is often at the base of much of the friction that we have in our lives. There is only one way to overcome pride and the friction it inevitably brings: We must submit to Jesus and His example of humility.

FOOD

Notice that David says, "He makes me to lie down in green pastures." He uses this picture to show how the Lord brings him to the state of rest and contentment by satisfying his spiritual hunger. Just as sheep will not lie down and rest unless they are well fed, neither will a Christian. If you look at a flock of sheep that is not well fed by their shepherd, you will notice that they are straggly and very nervous. They pace around, looking for any real food that might satisfy them. When a shepherd genuinely cares for his flock by leading them to the green pasture where they can eat to full satisfaction, their natural response is to lie down and rest in contentment. In the same way, God, in His goodness, has provided us with the full green pastures of His Word. He has raised up "shepherds" to rightly divide His truth and feed His flock to the point of satisfaction and peace.

Feeding on the Word

When I first came to know the Lord, I had such a hard time believing God loved me just the way I was. I remember many days of living in the tormenting anxiety that somehow I had lost my salvation, and it was now up to me to somehow earn it back. There were so many days filled with unrest, as I felt sure that if Jesus Christ returned, I would be left behind. Because of these thoughts, I was constantly trying to do things to earn God's favor that He might "give me back" my salvation and take me when He comes. I got over this by feeding on the good Word of God. As my pastor, Chuck Smith, taught verse-by-verse through the Book of Romans, I began to understand God's unconditional love for me. The more I was fed through this Book in the Bible, the more I understood the finished work of the cross. Thus, I was able to enter into the rest the Lord had for me as I fed upon the good Word of God.

I believe more pastors need to understand the unrest they are creating in the lives of the sheep by not feeding them a good diet of the Word of God. So often, these men are more worried about how to get more people into their churches than feeding the ones God has already placed under their care. Before He ascended into heaven, Jesus said to Peter, "If you love Me, feed My sheep."

Certainly, Jesus was telling Peter to feed His sheep to the point where they could rest in His love and the work of salvation He finished on their behalf. I think it is safe to say that you can have every other area in your Christian walk together; but, if you do not have a good grasp on the *finished* work of Jesus Christ at the cross, you will never enter into the rest God has for you. You will constantly be feeling that you must do something to earn your salvation and God's favor. You will be trying to add your feeble works to Christ's finished work when, in reality, there is nothing to add to it at all. To be able to fully enjoy the peace God has for us in our salvation, we must be able to rest in the unconditional love of Jesus Christ. This can only come about through being steadily fed God's Word.

The Word of God is the only place we can get a clear understanding of God's great love behind His free gift of salvation. Jesus said in Luke 12:32, "Do not fear, little flock, for it is your Father's good pleasure to give you the kingdom." Notice that He says, *"to give you the kingdom."* It is an absolutely free gift. I do not have to earn it, but receive it! I do not earn His love; I receive it. This is what we read about in 1 John 4:18, when he says, "...perfect love casts out fear...." We find this love repeatedly revealed in the green pastures of His Word.

Paul defines the kingdom of God in Romans: "The kingdom of God is righteousness and peace and joy..." (Romans 14:17). Jesus tells us to stop fearing, stop being full of anxiety, stop trying to work this thing out on our own, because it's God's good pleasure to give to us righteousness, peace, and joy. We need to let Him impart this to us as we get on the receiving end.

The Word feeds our spirits, fills our minds, and the end result is peace. That's why Paul says in Philippians, "...whatever things are true, whatever things are noble, whatever things are just,... pure,... of good report, if any virtue, anything praiseworthy—meditate on these things" (Philippians 4:8). A life that is full of the Word of God is full of peace.

41

FOLLOWING

David says, "He leads me beside the still waters." The secret of my peace is that I am the one who is being led.

In 1 Corinthians 11:1, Paul says, "Imitate me, just as I also imitate Christ." In Philippians 4:9, he says, "The things which you learned and received and heard and saw in me, these do, and the God of peace will be with you." What is he saying to us? *Learn to follow Jesus.*

Jesus is called the "Prince of Peace." The Word of God teaches that a Christian is to be characterized by peace. The way into peace is through prayer, humility, feeding on the Word of God, and following the Lord Jesus. This would all be wonderful if we would naturally and consistently follow right along behind the Lord. The only problem is that we tend to break the pattern of following by wandering off now and then. David says, "I am led to the waters of peace." But now and then there is a sheep who does not want to follow.

Jesus taught us that He has a way of handling that problem. He says in Matthew 18:12: "What do you think? If a man has a hundred sheep, and one of them goes astray, does he not leave the ninety-nine and go to the mountains to seek the one that is straying?" Jesus comes after us to bring us back to the place of following after Him. Though this parable is actually talking about salvation, I believe it applies continually—after we are saved—as well.

The Shepherd's Staff

It seems that within every flock there are always those who are prone to wander more frequently than others. For the sake of the sheep's well-being, a shepherd will take measures to chastise him to correct his behavior. Have you ever looked at a picture

42

of a shepherd and wondered what the curved staff in his hand was for? The curved part of the shepherd's staff has a number of uses, one of which is that of chastening a sheep who refuses to follow. The shepherd will take that staff and pop one of the sheep's legs, breaking it. Then he will set his leg and leave that sheep right there with all the others, in the midst of the green pastures, right by the still waters. He has done what is necessary to keep him there. By the time that little fellow heals, do you think he is going to be prone to wander any more? No! In a very similar way, the Lord works with us to keep us following Him.

Chastened to Follow

Some Christians fail to realize that our Good Shepherd *will* deal with us in similar ways. That is why it says in Hebrews that "no chastening seems to be joyful for the present." When God is disciplining you, it may feel like He is breaking your spiritual leg. Remember Jonah and the great fish? The Bible says the Lord prepared a great fish to swallow up Jonah. Sometimes He will use rather severe measures to bring us around.

I heard a well-known pastor tell how God used this process in his life when he was running from the Lord. One day, as he was driving down the highway at seventy miles an hour, he got into a accident. He was thrown from the car, painfully skidding down the highway on his back. The first thought that came into his mind as he bounced to a halt on the side of the road was, "Lord, what do you want me to do? [He actually said this.] "Big ministry, small ministry, I don't care—I will follow You."

The Lord has a way of teaching us how to surrender to Him and follow Him to the still waters.

Jesus speaks of the peace that comes to us when we follow Him. In Matthew 11:28-29, He says, "Come to Me, all you who labor and are heavy laden, and I will

43

give you rest. Take my yoke upon you and learn from Me, for I am gentle and lowly in heart, and you will find rest for your souls." He's not saying He will order circumstances in our lives to make things the way we like them. Sometimes it's just the opposite of that. But he will give us His peace, regardless of our circumstances, as we follow Him!

Peace Through Following

David Brainerd was a missionary to the Indians in North America. He provides a tremendous example of the peace we can have as we follow the Lord closely, even through the worst of circumstances:

"When news reached a notoriously ferocious tribe of Red Indians at the Forks of Delaware that a very pale 'paleface' was traveling alone in their direction, a group of them immediately set out to find him and kill him. Tracking their way swiftly and silently through the deep forests they knew so well, it was not long before they located him. The white stranger had erected his tent and was inside it. They crept up on him as soundlessly as shadows, their dark, cruel eyes fixed mercilessly on their prospective victim who was oblivious of their presence. The tall paleface was kneeling in prayer but an even deadlier enemy had beaten them to it. They watched with mixed feelings and bated breath as a rattlesnake slithered right up to the praying figure. It reared its vicious head and flicked out its forked tongue almost in his face—they waited for it to strike. Instead, to their amazement and for no apparent reason, it recoiled and retreated swiftly away through the brushwood.

"The Indians shook their heads in disbelief and retired just as silently and swiftly. Out of earshot they exclaimed in wonderment, 'The Great Spirit is with this paleface.'

"Unaware of the deadly enemies who had come within such close proximity of him, David Brainerd

44

continued praying, conscious only of being in the presence of Almighty God with a burden for the souls of the savage Indians whose nearby settlement he planned to visit the next day" (Colin Whittaker, *Seven Guides to Effective Prayer*, Minneapolis: Bethany House, 1987, p. 118).

We have a picture of a man who is in the midst of savage Indians whom he knows will seek his life. He is in the midst of wild animals, but we find him with perfect peace on his knees before the living God. We also find the protection of the living God around him. If you read the writings of David Brainerd, you will discover that he constantly talks about the presence of God in his life. He longed constantly for that private place of prayer that he might bask and dwell in the very presence of God Himself. He records how, through closely following the Lord, he found the peace of Jesus in his heart.

The Bible tells us in Isaiah 26:3, "You will keep him in perfect peace, whose mind is stayed on You, because he trusts in You."

What is the way into peace and rest? We begin by allowing the Good Shepherd to deal with our fears. He is faithful to do this as we come to Him in prayer. He will then seek to eliminate the friction with others that comes from our pride. As we submit ourselves to His example of humility and feed on His Word, following Him closely, we will be able to say with David: He makes me to lie down in green pastures, beside the waters of peace.

The Elements
of
Restoration

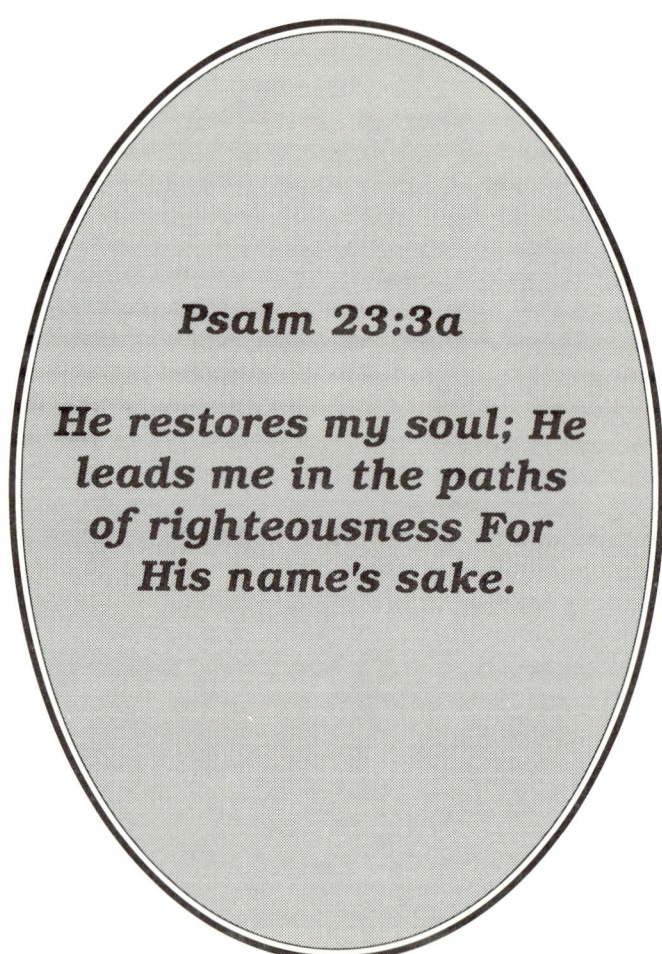

Psalm 23:3a

He restores my soul; He leads me in the paths of righteousness For His name's sake.

3

One of the most wonderful things in the Christian life is the way the Lord keeps us. Often we have wandered from His path, only to find His loving hands bringing us back into His sheepfold. In the book of Lamentations, Jeremiah has written these encouraging words: "Through the Lord's mercies we are not consumed, because His compassions fail not. They are new every morning; great is Your faithfulness" (Lamentations 3:22-23). It is by His faithfulness to restore our souls that we are able to continue with Him.

As David wrote, *"He restores my soul,"* he was probably reflecting on his own experiences of wandering and how often the Lord had brought him back. Although he does not elaborate in Psalm 23 on this subject of restoration, he has done so in Psalm 51. Thus, it will be of tremendous benefit to us in this chapter to look also at Psalm 51 as a commentary on the statement he has made about restoration.

There are basically two types of restoration we experience in the Christian life: one is *from* our sin and the other is *because of* our godly service.

OUR SIN

What does the word *restore* actually mean? We could define it: "to renew, refresh, rebuild, reclaim, reconstruct, recover, or revive." The basic way in which the Lord brings about this restoration has to do with our turning away from sin and its destructiveness and returning to satisfying fellowship with Him.

49

This is the process David is relating as he begins Psalm 51. He writes:

> Have mercy upon me, O God,
> According to Your lovingkindness;
> According to the multitude of Your tender mercies,
> Blot out my transgressions.
> Wash me thoroughly from my iniquity,
> And cleanse me from my sin.
>
> For I acknowledge my transgressions,
> And my sin is ever before me.
> Against You, You only, have I sinned,
> And done this evil in Your sight—
> That You may be found just when You speak,
> And blameless when You judge.
>
> Behold, I was brought forth in iniquity,
> And in sin my mother conceived me.
> Behold, You desire truth in the inward parts,
> And in the hidden part You will make me to know wisdom.
> Purge me with hyssop, and I shall be clean;
> Wash me, and I shall be whiter than snow....

These verses contain the elements of the process of restoration.

David, in deep distress, comes to God in repentance for the sin he had held in his heart for a year. According to his words in another Psalm, he experienced an intense inner agony as the hand of God was convicting him for his unrepented sin. David now asks the Lord to blot out his transgressions, that he might be restored to that glorious, love-filled relationship with God.

The lesson to learn here is that knowing about mercy will not help us unless we come to God and allow Him to personally cleanse us.

David had known of God's grace long before his sin with Bathsheba; however, he did not receive it until he confessed his sin and came to the Lord to receive the cleansing. It is in the context of this situation that he prays, "Wash me thoroughly from my iniquity, and cleanse me from my sin" (Psalm 51:2). He finally realized how his sin had separated him from God. Unrepented sin will bring a similar condition of blindness over a period of time to any child of God. In spite of this, Jesus Christ, the Good Shepherd, is longing to forgive and completely cleanse any and all who will personally come to Him for restoration.

Cleansing for the Honest Heart

Speaking to this issue, the apostle John penned these words, "But if we walk in the light as He is in the light, we have fellowship with one another, and the blood of Jesus Christ His Son cleanses us from all sin. If we say that we have no sin, we deceive ourselves, and the truth is not in us" (1 John 1:7-8). John reveals to us that when the heart is right, there is a continuous cleansing bringing an ongoing restoration.

We walk in the light as He is in the light by being honest with ourselves and with God.

This experience demands a move on our part to take responsibility for our sins. David understood this. In Psalm 51:3, he says, "For I acknowledge my transgressions, and my sin is ever before me. Against You, You only, have I sinned, and done this evil in Your sight." David is being open and honest about his sin, taking full responsibility for it. He has learned the hard way that sin brings chastisement. He is showing us that if we are to be restored, we must acknowledge our own sins by taking the responsibility for them.

Blaming Others

One thing that hinders us from doing this is our tendency to blame others for our faults. This character trait seems to have been inherited from Adam and Eve. After their fall in the garden, when God began to question Adam, he put the blame on Eve, and she tried to put the blame on the serpent (Genesis 3:12-13). And so it seems that we have the tendency to reach out and put the blame on someone else for either the bad circumstances in our lives, or our personal unhappiness. I have watched a great many people get full of anger, bitterness, and resentment as they refuse to be accountable to God in this matter. These people tend to go through their Christian lives unhappy most of the time, usually without understanding why. They are failing to see that those who do not take responsibility for their sins cannot be restored.

It is not at all unusual to find ourselves in the midst of a big cover-up operation before God because we want to put the blame on others. We deceitfully cover it up instead of simply bringing it to God openly, honestly, and responsibly. Confession is not always an easy thing to do, but it is much easier in the end than the chastisement we go through otherwise.

David fell into this trap when he sinned with Bathsheba. He covered it up, refusing to take responsibility for it. This went on for almost an entire year. He writes, after the fact, in Psalm 32:3-4, "When I kept silent, my bones grew old through my groaning all the day long. For day and night Your hand was heavy upon me; my vitality was turned into the drought of summer." He describes a horrible time of psychosomatic illness when he became so distraught within that he actually became physically sick. All of this was the result of covering up his sin. The Bible says, "He who covers his sins will not prosper, but whoever confesses and forsakes them will have mercy" (Proverbs 28:13). Why do we allow ourselves to fall into this trap of covering up?

There are a number of answers to that question, but one of the main reasons we try to cover up our sin is because we fail to see its destructiveness. We fail to realize how damaging sin can be. We look at sin and we think that we can manage it. We fail to realize that the effects of any one given sin are multiplied beyond what we are able to manage.

Spiders

The following example from nature illustrates this point: Many years ago, I lived on a farm. One day, while walking through the barn, I noticed a big spider hanging in its web in the corner. As I got closer, there was something that looked like a very tiny spider egg within a case about a quarter of an inch long, woven all around. At first glance, I assumed there was a baby spider inside. Looking more closely, I discovered that it was not a single egg with one spider inside, but that it was rather a colony of many little spiders that were just beginning to spring forth into life. There were what seemed to be multitudes of tiny spiders around the adult spider; and what I had thought was just one little egg was actually a cluster that had housed perhaps hundreds of eggs.

That colony of spiders is like a picture of the sin we tolerate in our lives. Left unconfessed, it becomes a colony of iniquity. "For he who sows to his flesh will of the flesh reap corruption..." (Galatians 6:8). What we think may be one little cluster in our lives can become a living mass of offense to God. Any given cluster of sin that is allowed to remain in our lives will issue forth in many other sins that can quickly become impossible to manage. It's like the old adage of one lie leading to another until you are caught in a web of lies which is beyond your control.

53

David Lost Control

That is what happened to David. He stood on his rooftop and lusted after Bathsheba in his heart. He did not deal with that one sin and, before it was all over, he broke four of the Ten Commandments. He broke the commandments not to covet, nor steal, nor commit adultery, nor murder. Four of the Ten Commandments were broken from one turning of the eyes and heart to gaze in the wrong direction. He did not deal with it, but covered it up, causing it to become completely unmanageable.

If we are to have restoration from our sin, it is imperative that we take full responsibility. We must come to the Lord in honesty, not blaming it on others. We are not to cover it up, but bring it to God in open confession and let Him deal with it. Confession for the Christian means "to come to an agreement with" Him about our sin. It actually involves coming to the place where you feel the same way about it that He does. It is absolutely vital that we all have the Holy Spirit to bring us to this condition of heart. Otherwise, we will have a "spider colony" going on within our lives with many unmanageable sins crawling out in every direction.

OUR SAVIOR

Thank God, we are not left alone to deal with our sin. We have a gracious, loving Savior who actively seeks us out to bring us back to Himself. Hence, David came to the Lord and asked Him to restore his joy, while acknowledging that God had used chastisement to bring him back: "Make me to hear joy and gladness, that the bones which You have broken may rejoice" (Psalm 51:8).

David realized that chastisement from God is actually a part of the restoration process. He refers to it, metaphorically, as the "bones which You have

54

broken," no doubt referring to a shepherd breaking the leg of a wandering lamb, as we saw in the last chapter. Chastisement is used by the Lord to draw us out from underneath our cover-up, back to an attitude of honest accountability. David articulated this even more clearly in Psalm 119:67, "Before I was afflicted I went astray, but now I keep Your word." This is not an enjoyable process; but, thank God, He does not leave us alone in our sin to wander endlessly. And what a blessing it is that, when we do come to the Lord, there is no limit to His great forgiveness.

His Great Forgiveness

David, speaking of the greatness of God's forgiveness, said, "Hide Your face from my sins, and blot out all my iniquities" (Psalm 51:9). If we will come to the Lord in honest confession, there isn't any sin that He won't forgive. In Isaiah 1:18, the Lord said, "'Come now, and let us reason together,' says the Lord, 'though your sins are like scarlet, they shall be as white as snow; though they are red like crimson, they shall be as wool.'" As we finally begin to reason with God about our sin and come to feel the same way about it as *He* does, the restoration comes.

Then David writes, in Psalm 51:10-12, "Create in me a clean heart, O God, and renew a steadfast spirit within me. Do not cast me away from Your presence, and do not take Your Holy Spirit from me. Restore to me the joy of Your salvation, and uphold me with Your generous Spirit." God forgives us immediately, but what we need is a total change of heart. The Lord has the ability and the grace to cleanse and forgive us, and then, even beyond that—to replace the sin with an actual righteousness in our hearts. That's the part that we so desperately need.

The Lord has the power to work that change into our lives, and the restoration we need can come only from our Savior. He is the One who does it; we cannot restore ourselves. Have you ever experienced falling into some sin in such a way that you simply cannot get back on your feet? The good news is that, if we will cry out to Him in those times, we have a Good Shepherd who will come and lift us back up to restore our souls.

The Cast-Down Sheep

Philip Keller, in his excellent book dealing with Psalm 23, has written of his experience with cast-down sheep. He writes about a cast-down sheep being one that has somehow ended up on its back and now has absolutely no ability to get itself back on its feet. There is only one hope for that sheep: his shepherd must find him and lift him back to an upright position. In his deeply heartwarming style, he explains this process:

"As soon as I reached the cast ewe my very first impulse was to pick it up. Tenderly I would roll the sheep over on its side. This would relieve the pressure of gasses in the rumen. If she had been down for long I would have to lift her onto her feet. Then straddling the sheep with my legs I would hold her erect, rubbing her limbs to restore the circulation to her legs. This often took quite a little time. When the sheep started to walk again she often just stumbled, staggered and collapsed in a heap once more.

"All the time I worked on the cast sheep I would talk to it gently, 'When are you going to learn to stand on your own feet?'—'I'm so glad I found you in time—you rascal!

"And so the conversation would go. Always couched in language that combined tenderness and rebuke, compassion and correction.

"Little by little the sheep would regain its equilibrium. It would start to walk steadily and surely. By and by it would dash away to rejoin the others, set free from its fears and frustrations, given another chance to live a little longer" (Philip Keller, *A Shepherd Looks at Psalm 23*, Grand Rapids: Zondervan, 1970, p. 63).

What a perfect picture of how our Good Shepherd leaves the ninety and nine to come and restore us, doing for us what we cannot do for ourselves.

Sharing with Others

After the Lord has restored us, He desires to use us in the process of reaching others. David writes, "Then I will teach transgressors Your way, and sinners shall be converted to You" (Psalm 51:13). David will be ready to reach out and restore others now that God has restored him.

Often we are trying to affect other people's lives when we ourselves need ministry. We need to be restored before we can pass it on. It has been said that *it takes free people to free people*; hence, *we* must first be restored.

When we have personally experienced the chastisement of God for our own sin and then the cleansing He brings, we have a powerful testimony in our lives which the Lord can use to reach others. There is nothing like the testimony of a changed life. This was the concept Jesus used in preparing Peter on the night of the Last Supper. When Jesus was ministering to the disciples, He said to him, "Peter, Satan has desired to sift you as wheat. He has desired to have you. But, Peter, I have prayed for you and when you are restored, or converted, or changed, then I want you to go forth and I want to use you to strengthen the brethren." Jesus was ministering this very principle to Peter, for He knew Peter was about to sin. He prepared him ahead of time for his impending fall, with the intent that he might be used to strengthen others after he was restored. God restores us so that we may come back into joyous fellowship with Him. When this has taken place, something very wonderful occurs in our hearts: a natural affection toward others returns.

Natural Affection

David prayed, "Do good in Your good pleasure to Zion; build the walls of Jerusalem" (Psalm 51:18). He was praying for his people that God would build them up. This is what happens to the restored heart when natural affection returns. There is a desire born within us to reach out and help people in need. The New Testament says the people outside of Jesus Christ are without natural affection. The Bible says the lack of natural affection will be one of the signs of the last days.

Does Anybody Care?

I used to live in New York City. I remember driving with a friend and stopping at a light with throngs of people passing by in front of us. We were trying to turn right but could not because of the crowd. Suddenly, a man began to assault a woman, trying to get her purse. While he was beating her up, everybody just kept marching by and ignoring her. That's what the Bible means when it says "without natural affection" (2 Timothy 3:3, King James Version). My buddy and I turned off the engine, jumped out of our truck, and ran toward the man. He saw us coming and ran. Natural affection is simply a real concern for your fellow man. David has had his heart restored. The natural affection that he has not had for a year, as he has been living in sin, has returned. Now he has a burden for those around him and he asks the Lord to build them up.

The Bible tells us in Romans 1:31 that men are without understanding, they are covenant breakers, they are without natural affection, they are implacable and unmerciful. But a restored soul has natural affection for others. This is why Paul wrote in Galatians 6:2, "Bear one another's burdens, and so fulfill the law of Christ." The natural affection that was lost in the fall in the garden of Eden is restored through the work of the Holy Spirit when our hearts are right with God and we have been restored.

OUR SERVICE

When our hearts are right, we are going to find ourselves entering into a pattern of serving and sacrificing. Moving on in Psalm 51, we read this truth: "Then You shall be pleased with the sacrifices of righteousness, with burnt offering and whole burnt offering; then they shall offer bulls on Your altar" (Psalm 51:19). He is praying for himself and his brethren that they may be strengthened, and that their hearts may give forth righteous sacrifices so that God will be pleased. Out of the restored soul comes a life of righteous service to others. That will lead us to the place where we will need a different kind of restoration: a restoration in order to go on dynamically serving the Lord. This is something we see repeatedly in the ministry of our Lord.

Mark 6:30-31 says, "Then the apostles gathered to Jesus and told Him all things, both what they had done and what they had taught. And He said to them, 'Come aside by yourselves to a deserted place and rest a while.' For there were many coming and going, and they did not even have time to eat." We have a beautiful picture of the Good Shepherd seeking to refresh the souls of the workers in His vineyard. It is so important, as we are working hard in the kingdom of God, that we take time out to rest. I think that sometimes we have a misconception that we have to "keep our noses to the grindstone" if we are going to be at all effective in the Lord's work. The truth is that, if we are not careful to turn aside and rest, we will become so fatigued that we will no longer be effective.

Edwin R. Roberts of Princeton Seminary once sat under a pastor who concluded his announcements to his congregation: "I am not going to take a vacation this summer; the devil never does." Roberts went home and re-read the Gospels to see what Jesus' attitude was on this issue. He found that of His three years' active ministry, there were mentioned ten periods of rest and retirement. This was in addition to the nightly rest and the Sabbath rest. We need to ask ourselves if we are going to follow the devil's example— or the Lord's.

Spurgeon's Rest

We do need rest from our service for the Lord. It seems there are those times when we hit the pillow that we feel as if we could sleep for three days. This is reminiscent of what happened to Charles Spurgeon. After speaking on one occasion to a gathering of 23,654 people in the Crystal Palace (in the days when there were no microphones or amplification systems) he returned home. The exertion of preaching to such a huge audience must have been great; although C. H. Spurgeon tells us that at the close of the day he did not feel conscious of any unusual fatigue. But that Wednesday night, he went to bed and slept continuously all through Wednesday night, all through Thursday, and on into Friday. All through Thursday, Mrs. Spurgeon went at intervals to look at her husband; but, finding him sleeping peacefully, she wisely let him rest until nature should be satisfied.

That was a man who slept for three days; he was tired. He needed rest from his sacrifice and service to the Lord.

Power to the Weak

In 1975, I went to Kodiak Island, Alaska, working to earn money to send to fellow missionaries. Because the purpose was solely to earn money, we often worked long hours, leaving us very fatigued at times. During that time, a dear saint took one of those little plant forms that grow on the sides of trees in Alaska and gave it to me with this verse inscribed on it: "Have you not known? Have you not heard? The everlasting God, the Lord, the Creator of the ends of the earth, neither faints nor is weary. There is no searching of His understanding. He gives power to the weak, and to those who have no might He increases strength. Even the youths shall faint and be weary, and the young men shall utterly fall, but those who wait on the Lord shall renew their strength; they shall mount up with wings like eagles, they shall run and not be weary, they shall walk and not faint" (Isaiah 40:28). That ministered to me so much then, and it ministers to me today. It speaks to me that God is able to restore my soul.

With Jesus Christ as our Good Shepherd, we can have that blessed confidence that, when necessary, He will leave the ninety and nine to seek us out and restore us. We can know with confidence His power to restore the weak. We can say, with gladness in our hearts: The Lord restores my soul.

Recognizing God's Voice

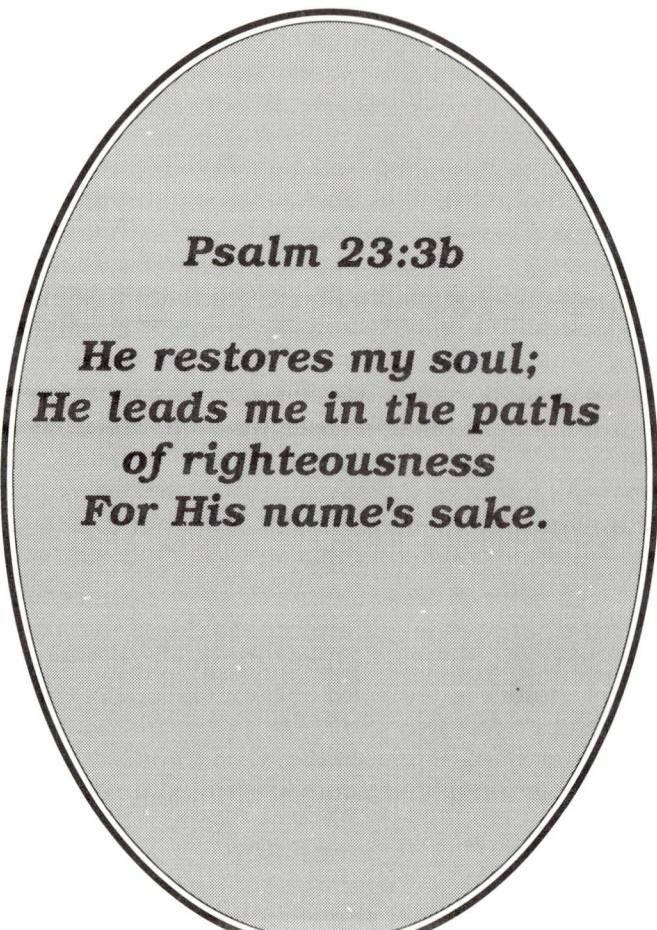

Psalm 23:3b

He restores my soul;
He leads me in the paths
of righteousness
For His name's sake.

4

There are many stories we hear of how the Lord guides and speaks to different people. I'll never forget the story I heard from a pastor who shared how he was talking to another pastor who told him how Jesus regularly appeared to him. Jesus, he claimed, was in the habit of appearing to him when he was shaving each morning. The first pastor responded, "I have only one question for you: How in the world do you keep on shaving?" To the other man's reply of, "Do you believe that He appears to me?" he answered, "No, I don't, but that doesn't bother me. What bothers me is that you believe it!"

If Jesus appeared to me while I was shaving, I don't know what I would do, but I do know that I would not keep on shaving. We hear so many testimonies from people about how the Lord has supposedly spoken to them or led them. We obviously cannot believe everything we hear, so we must discover what the Bible has to say about how God speaks to His people.

David writes, "He leads me in the paths of righteousness for His name's sake." In this chapter, we will examine *how* the Lord leads and speaks to us.

Where We Begin

To begin with, being led in the paths of righteousness and hearing the voice of God implies that we are submitted to Him and have given ourselves over to Him. We are depending upon Him for everything.

Proverbs 3:5-6 says, "Trust in the Lord with all your heart, and lean not on your own understanding;

in all your ways acknowledge Him, and He shall direct your paths." That is an absolute promise. If we will trust in Him, God has given His Word that He will lead us. Given the fact that we are trusting in Him, not trying to run our lives by our own power, then we are open to the great adventure of hearing the voice of God and seeing His guidance.

I do not want to be misunderstood. It is possible that Jesus could appear to you. He revealed Himself to Saul on the road to Damascus. It is also Biblically possible for an angel to appear to you, for the Bible says we do entertain angels while being unaware. It is also possible that you could receive a vision or a dream from God. But these are not the normal ways that God speaks to us on a daily basis. Normally, Jesus does not appear to you while you're shaving; normally, angels do not appear and talk to you. We do not get visions in the normal course of events. God does not usually talk to us in these ways.

I am opposed to the kind of Christianity that teaches that God is *constantly* appearing to people by means of Jesus, angels, visions, or dreams. That causes the rest of us to think that we are sub-citizens in the kingdom of heaven. I am not opposed to Biblical Christianity, but I am opposed to this other type of Christianity which has no basis in fact. In the Bible we see all of these things happen, but they happen decently, and they happen in order, and they are not everyday events. If it is in the Bible, I am open to it; but, if it is not in the Bible, I am not open to it—no matter what kind of a testimony is given. If we are to gain a solid, reasonable understanding of how the Lord leads us, we need to let the Word of God be our standard.

THE WRITTEN WORD

Let's begin to look at how the Lord leads us. David says, "He leads me in the paths of righteousness."

The first and most sure way the Lord speaks to us is through reading His written Word. The Bible is our Christian Life Manual, and it is there that we hear the voice of God in a very sure way. Basically, everything God has to say to us on any given issue is in the Bible. So the first place we go to have the Lord speak to us should be His Word. We simply sit down and read our Bibles with open hearts before the Lord. I find it helpful to always stop and pray before I begin, asking the Holy Spirit to give me wisdom in the knowledge of Him as I read.

Often, a new Christian will approach me after a service at our church and ask me, "As I read my Bible, is there anything in particular I am to be looking for? I'm having a hard time understanding it." My answer is always the same: "Just read it with an open heart. And the more you read, the more you will understand." When we are reading our Bibles on a daily basis over the course of months and years, we are primarily seeking to find out what God means by what He says, believing that God said what He meant and meant what He said; hence, taking the Bible literally. As we do this, we are building up a bank of knowledge. Our minds are like computers; they store everything as we read the Bible over a period of years. Over the process of time, the Word goes deeper and deeper, and the bank of knowledge fills up.

Help in a Crisis

I have a computer, and every time I get a new program for it, there is always a function called "Help..." If you're working through the program and you encounter a situation that you cannot solve on your own, you can hit an escape button and go to "Help...." In "Help...," you have pre-written advice on how to get out of the jam that you're in. That is exactly what we're talking about. Your mind is a computer; and if you feed it on the Word of God on a daily basis, reading the Bible for what it means by what it says in the context, you build up a bank of helpful knowledge. Then you step out to live God's program for your life. As you're living out God's program, sometimes you make a mess of it and enter into a crisis and you need help. You might say that the Holy Spirit presses the escape button and brings pre-written advice right to your heart to get you out of that situation. That "Help..." is the Word of God.

This is exactly the same truth Jesus speaks of when He says, "But the Helper, the Holy Spirit, whom the Father will send in My name, He will teach you all things, and bring to your remembrance all things that I said to you" (John 14:26). The primary way in which we understand God's guidance and hear His voice is through His written Word. That is the safest and most foolproof way to be led by the Lord.

One of the psalmists shares his testimony of being guided in this way when he writes in Psalm 119:54, "Your statutes have been my songs in the house of my pilgrimage." God's Word had guided and sustained him through the course of his pilgrimage through this life.

In Psalm 119:100, he says, "I understand more than the ancients, because I keep Your precepts." God's Word had filled him with the wisdom of heaven that takes us beyond the wisdom of this world.

Isaiah 28:13 says, "But the word of the Lord was to them, 'Precept upon precept, precept upon precept, line upon line, line upon line, here a little, there a little...'" The Lord went on to tell us through Isaiah, "Your ears shall hear a word behind you, saying, 'This is the way, walk in it...' " (Isaiah 30:21). Precept upon precept is the primary way that we learn and come into the guidance of God.

THE HOLY SPIRIT

After the Word of God, we are led by the Holy Spirit. I like to call this "charting the wind of the Holy Spirit." We find an example of this in sailing: When you sail from one part of the world to another in a sailboat, or any ship with sails, you must have charts which show the wind patterns. The trade winds are those which constantly blow in a certain direction and you must chart those winds if you are to get from A to Z. I like to think about the work of the Holy Spirit in that sense. Over the years, I see myself as charting the wind of the Holy Spirit. He works in my life by a number of ways. By reading the Bible and living out the Christian life, I've been "charting" His work by making footnotes and mental notes all along the way.

One of the ways the Holy Spirit works in our lives is by communicating the voice of God directly to our hearts. Our Lord explained this when He was teaching on the Holy Spirit in John 3:8: He said, "The wind blows where it wishes, and you hear the sound of it, but cannot tell where it comes from and where it goes. So is everyone who is born of the Spirit." Jesus clearly said that once we enter the realm of the Spirit, we enter into a process of movement and guidance of which the people outside of Christ have absolutely no awareness. He is talking about hearing the voice of God and being guided by it. In the next section, we will be looking at different ways the Holy Spirit works in our hearts to lead us in the paths of righteousness.

Application of the Bible

The first and most primary work of the Holy Spirit for us is to personalize the application of the Bible to our lives. As we saw earlier in this chapter, through reading the Bible, we will have that process of storing up God's Word in our hearts and in our minds. But it

69

is through the inspiration of the Holy Spirit that God's Word actually comes to life for us.

Have you ever been reading your Bible and, all of a sudden, something seems to leap off the page at you? I like to call that "the popcorn effect." That's when you're personally reading your Bible and a verse pops out to you. It seems to open up and truth starts going in every direction—applying directly to you. That is the work of the Holy Spirit. He comes along and opens the Word of God to you in a personal way. This is different from just storing up the knowledge in your heart that the Spirit might use later.

In Psalm 119:18, the psalmist says, "Open my eyes, that I may see wondrous things from Your law." When I come to the Bible, I always pray that the Holy Spirit will open my eyes and give me that personal application that I need to live out my life today.

We also experience this type of thing during the teaching of the Word of God when the Holy Spirit is at work to apply it in a personal way. This is a little different from the popcorn effect, although that does also happen during sermons.

During sermons, I find very often that I get what I like to call "the knife-in-the-heart effect." We are told in the Book of Hebrews that the Word of God is sharper than a two-edged sword, and is able to discern between the· thoughts and intents of the heart. There you are, just calmly, innocently sitting and listening to the teaching of the Word of God, when a statement suddenly cuts deep into your heart. This is the place where, if I am listening to a tape, I always stop the tape player and back it up. I want to hear it again, because I realize the Lord is really talking to me. If there is enough of this occurring in a message, it will result in another wonderful phenomenon:

When you hear a sermon and everybody afterwards seems to think that the message was directed personally to them, I call that "the that-was-for-me effect." That's the work of the Holy Spirit. There is no way that any man could stand up and teach from one Book and have everybody think that it's just for them. That is definitely the voice of God speaking to their hearts. Don't assume that the pastor happens to know what you have been going through; assume that God is talking to you—and then take it seriously enough to act upon it.

One time a wife, who was separated from her backslidden husband, talked him into coming to a Bible study I was teaching. I barely even knew this individual or any of the details of his life. On the way home from the study, he became very angry with his wife, saying, "What is the big idea of telling that pastor all the secrets of my life! How could you be so deceitful as to invite me to a message that was prepared beforehand with the details of my sinful life in mind!" It took the rest of the evening for the woman to convince her husband that she had not spoken to me beforehand. The truth is that the Holy Spirit, who knows all of the secrets of everyone's heart, was applying the Word of God to him.

Spirit's Conviction

Another way the Holy Spirit works is through conviction. Conviction is the light of God shining on our hearts, showing us that He wants to deal with a specific area. This produces a feeling that we are in the presence of God, and He knows exactly where we are. When God beams His light, it is like darkness being peeled back. It seems as though, suddenly, there is a heavenly searchlight beaming down on this given area of our lives.

Paul writes in Ephesians 5:11-17: "And have no fellowship with the unfruitful works of darkness, but rather expose them. For it is shameful even to speak of those things which are done by them in secret. But

71

all things that are exposed are made manifest by the light, for whatever makes manifest is light. Therefore He says: 'Awake, you who sleep, arise from the dead, and Christ will give you light.' See then that you walk circumspectly, not as fools but as wise, redeeming the time, because the days are evil. Therefore do not be unwise, but understand what the will of the Lord is."

Paul is talking about the light of God exposing something in our hearts and lives. We are to stop walking like the people in the world. Therefore, see that you walk uprightly and be filled with the Spirit.

Conviction is a vital work of the Holy Spirit. We need to recognize and respond when it comes upon our hearts. At this point, some reader is probably wondering, "Wait! What is the difference between feeling the conviction of the Holy Spirit and condemnation?" Conviction is totally different from condemnation.

Condemnation is feeling guilty and discouraged when you have sinned. It usually leaves you thinking, "What's the use! I can't make it in the Christian life. I think I'll just give up." That is condemnation. Conversely, when conviction comes and the Holy Spirit shines the light on your heart, there's always encouragement behind it —never discouragement. The Holy Spirit never ever discourages; the devil does that.

The Holy Spirit speaks to our hearts by conviction. It is important at this point to realize that you will feel, sense, and hear the voice of the Holy Spirit when your heart is soft and pliable. Something that can hinder this process greatly is sin. Sin always hardens your heart. If you're living in sin, you're going to have a hard heart; sin always deafens our ears to the voice of God. The more closely we walk with the Lord, the more sensitive we are to His guidance through conviction.

Quick Impression

Another way is through a quick, clear impression. This is what happened to Philip in Acts 8:29. Philip went down to Gaza, and the Bible says, "Then the Spirit said to Philip, 'Go near and overtake this chariot.'" The Holy Spirit led Philip to the Ethiopian eunuch. As a result of the Spirit's leading, there was a wonderful ministry that took place with this man. The Lord leads us in this way, very often, on a daily basis.

One time, while I was driving down a California freeway, my mind was wandering on a variety of subjects. As I was in the middle of a conversation with the Lord, a quick, clear impression cut through to the core of my heart. I felt that the Lord was saying that He wanted me to see about getting on the radio one day a week. I admit being very surprised about it, because I had not thought about the possibility of a radio ministry for many months. But suddenly that impression was there in my heart.

Once you've been walking with the Lord long enough, depending on Him, and not leaning on your own understanding, you begin to recognize when it is the voice of God. I began to wait on Him to make certain He might clarify it to my heart. When you think the Holy Spirit is speaking to you, it's good to ask somebody if they have a witness about it. I came home and told my wife, Cindy, that I thought God had spoken to me while driving down the freeway about getting on the radio one day a week. She had the witness in her heart that it was the Lord's leading and, within a few weeks' time, we were indeed on the radio one day a week.

Deep, Sustained Impression

God also speaks through a deep, sustained impression. This is when the Lord is calling you to some new,

73

specific ministry. He wants a major shift or a whole new avenue in your life, and He begins to deeply impress this burden upon your heart. Our ministry first went on the radio one day a week as a result of that quick, deep impression. Then the Lord began to set in my heart a deep, sustained impression that we were to go on five days a week. At the time, that seemed totally unreasonable and out of the question. I began to pray about it and the burden stayed there, crystal clear. It never went away, from one day to the next. Finally, I felt that the Lord was impressing upon my heart that the time was approaching. I felt the Lord was saying, "I want you to call the manager of this station and tell him about this burden." I did, and the manager laughed, saying that they rarely had an opening on the prime time slot I was talking about. Nevertheless, within about a month, we were on the radio five days a week! That was the hand of God. How did it all come about? It came as a result of "sustained burden" upon my heart. I remember being open at the time to waiting on the Lord for five or ten years for Him to bring that burden to pass. I just left the situation in the hands of God, not realizing how quickly He was planning on working it out. If you're not leaning on your own understanding, you have the flexibility to do that. If you're in a hurry to make something come to pass in your life, if you're trying to build your Christian life, if you're trying to do it on your own—then you're going to have a lot of problems with this. But, if you're resting in the Lord, it is a joy to let Him work things out on His timetable.

Restless Spirit

Another way the Spirit leads is through a restless spirit. This is similar to conviction, but it is not the same because it generally doesn't deal with sin. Conviction deals with sin, but this is a restlessness in your spirit when the Lord is wanting to give you some specific guidance. You may be moving in the wrong direction and, as you're moving that way, you're getting more and more restless. This is exactly what happened to Paul in Acts 16:7: "After they had come to Mysia, they tried to go into Bithynia, but the Spirit did not permit them." The Lord used a restless spirit to guide him in this way until he received the vision of the man from Macedonia. As a result, he went on to pioneer a church in Philippi, which he otherwise probably would never have founded.

The classic example of this in the Old Testament is in the Book of Esther. A wicked man, named Haman, had devised a plan to have Mordecai, a man of God, killed. He had developed a cruel plan and had gone so far as to build a gallows on which to hang him. He had even convinced the king of his plan; but the Bible says: "That night the king could not sleep. So one was commanded to bring the book of the records of the chronicles; and they were read before the king. And it was found written that Mordecai had told of Bigthana and Teresh, two of the king's eunuchs, the doorkeepers who had sought to lay hands on King Ahasuerus. Then the king said, 'What honor or dignity has been bestowed on Mordecai for this?'... And the king said, 'Who is in the court?' Now Haman had just entered the outer court of the king's palace to suggest that the king hang Mordecai on the gallows that he had prepared for him" (Esther 6:1-4).

God had sent a restless spirit to the king. Because he wasn't able to sleep, he found out that Mordecai was a hero; hence, he made the decision to decorate and exalt him. This ruined Haman's entire plan and, as a result, Mordecai's life was saved. All of that came about as a result of a restless spirit. One of the greatest "red flags" to look for, as you're moving forth in your Christian life, is a restless spirit .

This is one of the ways in which God has worked with my wife, Cindy, and me. One of our greatest series of chain-reaction miracles came about as a result of a restless spirit. We were living in Fountain Valley at the time, renting a house. The man who owned the house sold it and gave us a thirty-day notice. We had already been looking for months and months to rent another house. Finally, we had only thirty days left and we still hadn't found one. We found places we liked and filled out the forms, but they would always be rented to someone else. Through a series of events, we were on our way, driving down the freeway with an appointment to rent a condominium which we did not want to rent.

All of a sudden, we were restless—and it was obvious that something was wrong. We decided to get off on another off-ramp and look for a place in a different city: Laguna Hills. They were building out there and we went to see about buying our own home; yet we had no money in the bank, and could not qualify to buy anything. We drove down to Laguna Hills to some brand new town homes. We walked into the office and a lady came up, holding the price sheet. It all looked very expensive to me, so I told my wife that we were in the wrong place. To my surprise, she ignored me and told the lady that we were interested in buying one of the houses. To make a long story short, they got us in with only five percent down—which we did not even have. The Lord then brought a man along who loaned us the down payment, and we moved in.

The home went up quickly in value, which worked out another problem that developed: we had a surprise daughter. Everything was fine in the town house until number three came along. We were not planning to have three. Diana burst on the scene and this house, which had been perfect, was not perfect any more. By this time, I needed an office at home for study, because our congregation was growing rapidly and the phone was beginning to ring constantly in the church office.

We qualified for the loan on a new home where I now have an office and twice as much room. It all started with a restless spirit by that off-ramp on the freeway. This is how the hand of God works in our lives. Furthermore, the lady who processed the new home loan told us our name sounded familiar. She asked if she had processed another loan for us and we said, "Yes, the one on the town home." She told us that when we qualified for that original loan, it was a miracle. She had never seen anything like it before or since. We thought it was, too! You never know what will happen if you respond to that restless spirit in the way the Lord wants you to.

To conclude this story, the homes that we moved into were done with a priority list because of the housing shortage at the time. That means that you are eligible to purchase a home according to where your name is on the list. There were nine hundred people on the list; we ended up number twenty. That was the hand of God. God is real and He is working in our lives. When He gives us a restless spirit, we need to respond; we never know where He's going to take us!w

Deep Peace

We see the Lord speaking to us by conviction, by a quick impression, by a sustained impression on our hearts, and by a restless spirit. A fifth thing would be what I would call a deep peace. In Philippians 4:6-7, Paul writes, "Be anxious for nothing, but in everything by prayer and supplication, with thanksgiving, let your requests be made known to God; and the peace of God, which surpasses all understanding, will guard your hearts and minds through Christ Jesus." The original language implies "a garrison will stand guard around your heart." If you will come and offer your request to God and seek Him for guidance, He will garrison your heart with peace and move you along in that realm of peace. That is one of the great ways God speaks to us.

This is the way I know what to leave in and what to leave out of my sermons. I ask the Lord for guidance in preparing messages. You have information stacked up and then realize you could talk for three days on this subject. You get to the point where you wonder what to leave in and what to take out. The only way I know is by the peace in my heart. I'll just go right down the page of all my notes and if I have a peace, I'll leave it. If I feel a little restless about leaving it in, then I'll pull it out. I don't even think twice if I have the slightest bit of restlessness—I yank it out; it's not for God's people. This is peace in your heart.

My wife, Cindy, and I went to buy a car one day. We went to a dealership and were looking at the various models. We drove one around and when we decided we liked it, we sat down to buy it. Up until that point, I had been feeling very peaceful. But suddenly, I became very restless. The peace I had up to that point was gone. I told Cindy that I had lost all my peace. Based upon the fact that I no longer had a peace in my heart, we thanked them for their time and walked out. For many years since then, I have thanked the Lord that I did not buy that car. It would have been a very bad financial move for us.

You must follow the peace in your heart, especially on major decisions in your life.

DREAMS AND VISIONS

In Acts 2:17, Peter, filled with the Holy Spirit, began to quote Scripture, a prophecy from Joel: "And it shall come to pass in the last days, says God, that I will pour out of My Spirit on all flesh; your sons and your daughters shall prophesy, your young men shall see visions, your old men shall dream dreams." It does not necessarily have to happen with the daughters prophesying, the young men receiving the visions, and only the old men getting the dreams: it probably passes around to everybody. The Lord is saying that, in the last days, people will have prophecies, visions, and dreams. It's black and white. It's not a mystical thing. God can and does speak in all those ways.

After the apostle Paul had the restless spirit that kept him from going into Bithynia, the Bible says: "And a vision appeared to Paul in the night. A man of Macedonia stood and pleaded with him, saying, 'Come over to Macedonia and help us'" (Acts 16:9). The vision gave him the guidance he needed. God does give visions today and when they are truly from Him, they are very helpful; but they don't come every single day in our lives.

The Lord also speaks to us in dreams. He spoke to Joseph in a dream, showing him to get out of Bethlehem and away from Herod. When they were in Egypt, he received another dream that told him to go back. I am confident that the Lord can do the same today with any one of us if He so desires. But don't think every dream you ever have is a message from God. Though we see God speak through dreams throughout Scripture, they are not the average way God communicates to His people.

THROUGH OTHER PEOPLE

As He is leading us through all of the means we have looked at so far in this chapter, God will also speak to us through other people. This could be in many different ways. He sent a man named Ananias to Paul while Paul was still blind from his conversion on the Damascus Road. God came to Ananias, gave him a vision, and then sent him off to talk to Paul: "...he said, 'Brother Saul, the Lord Jesus, who appeared to you on the road as you came, has sent me that you may receive your sight and be filled with the Holy Spirit'" (Acts 9:17). God was speaking to Paul through another person.

79

I think this happens to us quite often. God is speaking to you and you are ignoring it. You have heard it over and over, and perhaps have a sustained burden about it. Finally, someone will come to you and say something that will cut like a knife in your heart. It will seem that they are speaking right to your heart, even though they are not even remotely aware of the details of your life. Sometimes this will occur in an off-handed way. At other times, they will know they have a message for you. God speaks to us through other people, and He does that with the "word of wisdom" (a gift of the Holy Spirit as recorded in 1 Corinthians 12), the "word of knowledge," and "prophecy."

A word of wisdom is like what Solomon says, "A word fitly spoken is like apples of gold in settings of silver" (Proverbs 25:11). Thus, if you're in a quandary or a crisis, not knowing which way to turn, and somebody comes to you with a few words that seem to settle everything into the right perspective, you have possibly received a word of wisdom.

I even look for it in off-the-cuff remarks. Once you get used to the fact that God speaks in all these ways, you will find yourself walking around with one ear open all the time.

CIRCUMSTANCES

Circumstances would be another way to hear God's voice, as He sovereignly arranges the situations of your life. Usually, when the Lord is leading in a specific direction, the circumstances around you will verify that. However, I must hasten to add that sometimes, after you have become clearly convinced that God is leading you in a certain direction, the devil will bring a set of circumstances your way to sidetrack you away from God's plan. Watch and pray on that one.

ANGELS

A last possibility would be angels. An angel might appear to you. I've never seen an angel in my life; I don't even know anybody who has seen an angel; but an angel could appear to you. Angels appeared all the way through the Bible. They are ministers sent to those who are heirs of salvation. Be open to these things.

These are the ways that God speaks. It isn't mystical; it's crystal clear in the Bible that He speaks in all of these ways. But, primarily, He speaks to us through His Word, by the Holy Spirit to our hearts, through others, and through circumstances. Out of everything we have looked at, these are the four primary ways that God speaks to us. Watch for them.

It is a magnificent incentive to me to walk closely to the Lord, so that I might hear His voice in as many of these ways as possible. Don't be discouraged if you haven't heard the Lord's voice in all of these ways; it all takes time.

"Trust in the Lord with all your heart, and lean not on your own understanding; in all your ways acknowledge Him, and He will direct your paths." His promise is that, as you do, you will hear the voice of God through the impressions He makes on your heart. It is in these ways that He leads us in the paths of righteousness for His name's sake.

Where He Leads Me

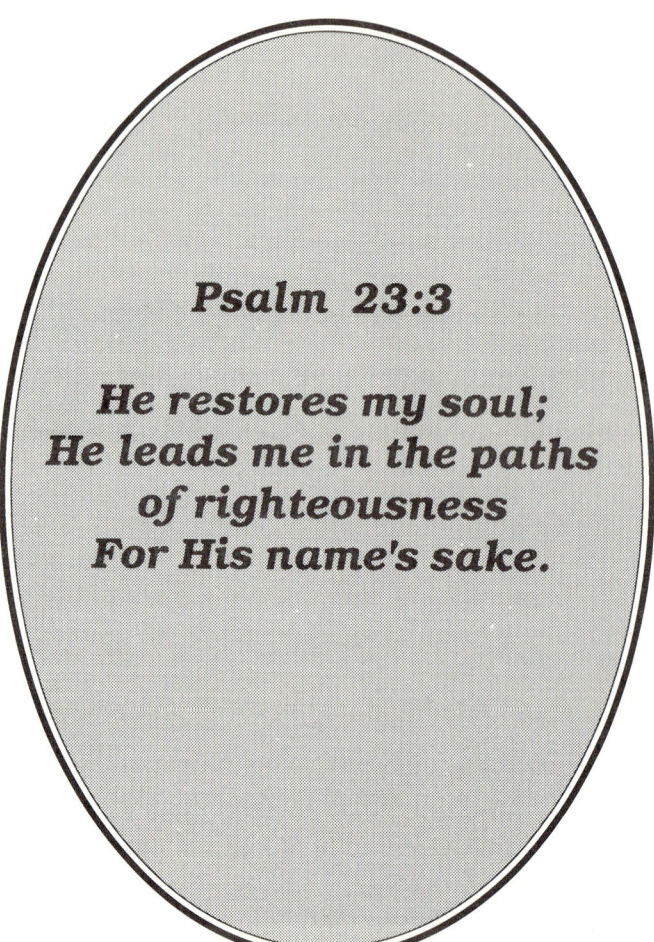

Psalm 23:3

He restores my soul;
He leads me in the paths
of righteousness
For His name's sake.

5

The Bible teaches that the knowledge of God is fathomless; we will never know all there is to know about the Lord, for His ways are past finding out. The Christian life is one long great adventure. In a very real sense, this is what we are talking about in terms of the Lord leading us in the paths of righteousness. If the Lord leads me in the paths of righteousness, where exactly does He lead me? Where are those paths leading?

Paths of righteousness could literally be translated "the right path." We could say He leads us to go the right way in the plan He has for our lives. To put it another way, the things of God are simple and the Lord knows how weak and how helpless we are. We have proven it to Him over and over by our behavior. Knowing our weakness on the one hand, and having a clear plan for us on the other, the Lord has promised that if we will simply follow Him, He will be very faithful to lead us in the direction we are to go.

A Plain Path

Psalm 16:11 says, "You will show me the path of life; in Your presence is fullness of joy; at Your right hand are pleasures forevermore."

In Psalm 27:11 we read, "Teach me Your way, O Lord, and lead me in a smooth path, because of my enemies." Our enemies are without number; we fight the host of hell on a daily basis. There is not a day that goes by that we are not in some kind of spiritual warfare. We wrestle with the world; we wrestle with our own hearts; and we need a plain path cut right through the midst of our enemies.

Proverbs 4:18 says, "But the path of the just is like the shining sun, that shines ever brighter unto the perfect day." If we will follow the Lord closely, living an upright life, not only will He guide us, but this promise in the Proverbs says that the guidance will become clearer, and the light will become brighter and brighter as we move along. That is why many of the efforts of the enemy are targeted toward this truth. He wants us to believe that we cannot grow any further. We will examine the main areas in our lives where we can confidently expect to receive clear guidance from the Lord.

SEEKING HIM

To begin with, the Lord leads us in the paths of righteousness in our seeking of Him. As we seek Him, there are a few key things we need to keep in mind which will help us to receive and follow His guidance. These things may seem to be basic; yet, if they are not taking place, then we cannot truly claim to be seeking Him. Also, if these disciplines are lacking in our walks, it will greatly hinder—if not bring to an entire halt—the other very important issues we will be looking at later in this chapter.

Be Willing

Often, individuals desiring the benefits of God's guidance in their lives overlook one very important basic issue: The Lord leads us when we are ready to be led His way. An example of this is the rich young ruler. He fell at Jesus' feet and seemed, at first impression, to have a sincere desire to be led in the paths of righteousness. He asked, "Good Master, what must I do to inherit eternal life?"

(Matthew 19:16). But the answer was not what he wanted to hear. The Bible says that "he went away sorrowful" (Matthew 19:22). He was not willing to do what Jesus told him to do. Although the Lord has a rich, comprehensive plan waiting for us, He cannot impart it to us until the day comes when we are absolutely willing to go His way. In the case of the rich young ruler, he missed out on salvation as well as guidance. In the case of many of those who already possess eternal life, they miss out by coming to the Lord without being willing to do *anything* the Lord might ask, and they also go away sorrowful. A willing heart is the first step.

Be Waiting and Praying

Once we are willing, we need to make sure that we are waiting and praying. This is difficult because, after we become willing, we quickly begin to get excited. Once the Lord has worked in our hearts to the point where we can say with David, "Search me, O God, and know my heart; try me, and know my anxieties; and see if there is any wicked way in me, and lead me in the way everlasting" (Psalm 139:23-24); once we come to the place of full, open disclosure before the Lord, we want things to happen right away. That is exactly when we need to slow down and wait. We must stop and wait if we are to hear the voice of God and gain the direction we need to go forward in the paths of righteousness. There must be a waiting.

The same David who writes: search me, try me, and lead me, is also the one who writes, "Wait on the Lord; be of good courage..." (Psalm 27:14). In Psalm 37:34, he says, "Wait on the Lord, and keep His way, and He shall exalt you to inherit the land..." In Psalm 123:2, "Behold, as the eyes of servants look to the hand of their masters, as the eyes of a maid

87

to the hand of her mistress, so our eyes look to the Lord our God..."

We come willing and then we wait, because we can get ourselves into trouble when we get this initial zeal. It is through waiting and praying that we place ourselves in a position to clearly hear the voice of God.

Be Reading

While we are waiting, we need to be reading the Bible. Psalm 119:105 says, "Your word is a lamp to my feet and a light to my path."

It is said that when Martin Luther was asked to sign a copy of the German Bible he had translated, he wrote: "Therefore let this book in which He speaks to you be commended to you. For He did not cause it to be written to no purpose. He never meant for us to let it lie there in neglect as if He were speaking to the mice under the bench where it is lying, or to lie there on the pulpit—open, unused—speaking to the flies that come nearby! We are to read it, to think about it, to study it—certain that He Himself *is speaking with us in it.*"

God speaks through His Word. If you want to hear the voice of God, read while you are waiting. If you arc reading the Bible, you are going to be throwing wood constantly on the fire of your prayer life. If you are not reading the Bible, but just desiring a prayer life, the fire is going to go out. With both together, you will begin to hear the voice of God and get ready for action.

Be Watching

Seeking the Lord to be led in the paths of righteousness involves much more than simply coming to God and saying, "I'll go Your way!" By very definition it involves: being willing, waiting, reading, and praying. When we reach this point, we need to do one last thing—start watching. Start watching, because God is going to start working. This is where it begins in terms of being led in the paths of righteousness; as we seek Him, we get these things lined up.

As we are doing all of this we are going to discover the mind of God and receive the divine guidance that we need.

If you are only praying, you are not going to receive it. If you are only reading, you are not going to receive it. If you are only waiting, you are not going to receive it. All of these things must be working together for you to receive all that you need from the Lord.

It has been said that Bible study alone without prayer will produce a Pharisee. But prayer alone, without a knowledge of God's Word, will produce a fanatic; there are no boundaries, no control. Thirdly, if you simply watch the circumstances—without the prayer and without the reading—then you will become a fatalist. You'll be a person who looks around at the circumstances and says, "What will be, will be."

Rather, we must have *all* of these things. We need to be reading the Bible, gaining the guidance, praying, bringing in the fire, and then watching the circumstances. When we get to that place, we will be in the process of being led in the paths of righteousness.

If we are walking in that place, we can safely be assured that we will never lack the blessing of God. It's that simple.

SANCTIFICATION

The Lord leads me as I seek Him. Second, He leads me in the paths of righteousness, and that speaks of sanctification: leaving the old path and walking on a new path or, you could more accurately and specifically say, living a holy life.

If the Lord is going to lead us in the paths of righteousness, that implies that we had other paths we used to walk on. Before we came to Jesus Christ, there were deep, well-worn paths that we used to tread. You could also call them habits. In a very real sense, before you come to Christ, your life is a network of habits. I see sanctification as the Lord leading us into new habits of holiness. This is not simply the idea of becoming a moral person; it is much deeper.

The Morality Issue

Holiness or sanctification is something that happens from the inside out. A moral man who looks good on the outside may have morality; but morality is not holiness. There are people who do not know God in even the remotest way; but, because of the way they were raised, they live moral lives. They live outwardly clean lives. Holiness is inward. If you have holiness, then you are not doing wrong inwardly—within your heart. A moral man may not commit sin on the outside; but a holy man will not commit sin on the inside—in his heart. There is a big difference between the two. A holy man, if he does commit sin on the inside, will weep over it. That is the difference. When we talk about sanctification, we are not speaking about getting the outside together; we are talking about getting our hearts upright before the Lord in holiness.

Holiness is a very serious issue in the Christian life. Ephesians 4:24 says, "and that you put on the new man which was created according to God, in righteousness and true holiness." Because this is a command, it follows that God has given us the divine enablement by His Holy Spirit necessary to live out that command. In 2 Corinthians 7:1 Paul writes, "Therefore, having these promises, beloved, let us cleanse ourselves from all filthiness of the flesh and spirit, perfecting holiness in the fear of God." Just how serious is the issue of holiness in the Word of God and in the Christian life? The Bible says, "Pursue peace with all men, and holiness, *without which no one will see the Lord* " (Hebrews 12:14, emphasis added).

Personal Holiness

There is a wonderful old book called *The Reformed Pastor* that was written in 1656 by a Puritan named Richard Baxter. He has written these challenging, stimulating words concerning our sanctification:

"Brethren, we are exhorted to take heed to ourselves, lest we live with those actual sins which we may preach against in others. Let us see that we are not guilty of that which we may daily condemn.

"Will we make it our work to magnify God? And when we have done so, do we dishonor Him as much as others? Will we proclaim Christ's governing power? And yet when we have spoken of this power, do we deny it, and rebel ourselves? Will we preach God's laws and willfully break them? If sin be evil, why then do we live in it?

"If there be no sin, then why do we dissuade men from it? If it be dangerous, how dare we venture on it! If it does not exist, how dare we tell men it does so? If God's threatenings be true, why do we not fear them? If they are false, why do we trouble men needlessly with them and make them frightened without a cause?

"Do you not know the judgment of God? That they who commit such things are said to be worthy of death, and yet we would persist in doing them? (Romans 1:32). You who teach others, will you not teach yourselves? You who say a man should not

91

commit adultery, or be drunk or be covetous—are you such yourself? You who make your boasts in the law—do you not realize that in breaking the law you dishonor God? (Romans 2:21-23).

"What! Shall the tongue speak evil that also speaks against evil? Shall it censure and slander and secretly backbite while it cries down these behaviors and the like in others? Take heed then to yourselves, lest you cry down sin and yet do not overcome it in yourself. For as 2 Peter 2:19 reminds us, of whom a man is overcome, of the same he is brought into bondage. To whom you yield yourselves servants to obey, his servants you are whom you obey—whether of sin unto death, or of obedience unto righteousness (Romans 6:16)." (Richard Baxter, *The Reformed Pastor*, Portland, Ore.: Multnomah Press, 1982, pp. 28-29).

Holiness is a serious issue in the Christian life. And it's easy to judge sin with your mouth. It's easy to judge it in the lives of others while walking in another direction yourself. Yet the Lord has given us the power to live out the things that are in His Word; it is the power of the Holy Spirit.

By His Spirit

In the church of today, so many have been overtaken by apathy, indifference, or lukewarmness. So many seem to be satisfied with salvation and care so little about sanctification.

In a classic work called *The Knowledge of the Holy,* A. W. Tozer writes: "Quite literally a new channel must be cut through the desert of our minds to allow the sweet waters of truth that will heal our great sickness to flow in....

"Only the Spirit of the Holy One can impart to the human spirit the knowledge of the holy....

"This holiness God can and does impart to His children. He shares it with them by imputation and by impartation, and because He has made it available to them through the blood of the Lamb, He requires it of them. To Israel first and later to His Church God spoke, saying, 'Be ye holy; for I am holy.' He did not say 'Be ye as holy as I am holy,' for that would be to demand of us absolute holiness, something that belongs to God alone. Before the uncreated fire of God's holiness angels veil their faces. Yea, the heavens are not clean, and the stars are not pure in His sight. No honest man can say 'I am holy,' but neither is any honest man willing to ignore the solemn words of the inspired writer, 'Follow peace with all men, and holiness, without which no man shall see the Lord.'

"Caught in this dilemma, what are we Christians to do?...

"By faith and obedience, by constant meditation on the holiness of God, by loving righteousness and hating iniquity, by a growing acquaintance with the Spirit of holiness [by that and that alone], we can acclimate ourselves to the fellowship of the saints on earth and prepare ourselves for the eternal companionship of God and the saints above" (A. W. Tozer, *The Knowledge of the Holy,* San Francisco: Harper and Row, 1961, pp. 104-107).

The real joy in the Christian life begins as we come out from among the ways of the world to walk in the paths of righteousness, in intimate companionship with God as a people who walk worthy of His holy name. At this point we are then prepared for the next step in being led in the paths of righteousness: our service unto the Lord. This involves following in the footsteps of Jesus.

SERVICE

If we are to walk in the footsteps of Jesus, then we need to make Him our primary role model. The Bible says in 1 John 2:6, "He who says he abides in Him ought himself also to walk just as He walked." We need, literally, to follow in the footsteps of Jesus. He is our role model—the Standard for the Christian life. We inevitably lower the standard by initially following some man or woman, and then comparing ourselves with them. We need to read through the Gospels very carefully, to watch as Jesus ministers. We need to watch what He does, how He interacts with people, how He responds to sin, and how He responds to hurt and to need.

I think it is extremely helpful to have other Christians in our lives as secondary role models of true spiritual service, but we need to make certain that Jesus is our main role model. Then we can safely let the Lord lead us to those who can truly be secondary real-life role models worth following. The apostle Paul said, "Be followers of me, even as I also am of Christ." He identified the fact that all of us have a very real need for a living, flesh-and-blood example in the faith.

Spiritual Heroes

A number of years ago a very well-known pastor was speaking at a pastors' conference. This man has spoken all over the world and has written many books. All of the pastors were listening and interacting in a discussion on things like "hermeneutics," "homiletics," and Biblical "exegesis." When they had finished going through all of this and came to the end of the conference, there was a time set aside for questions and answers. Someone asked the speaker about his heroes. Whom did he pattern himself after? Who is it that has been an inspiration to cause him to preach like this? The fact is that the speaker himself was the role model of many of the men in that group, and they wanted to know how he had gotten to where he was. That tells us that we have a desperate need deep within our hearts for a role model— someone tangible, somebody we can see, reach out to and touch.

We need to be very careful that our role model is submitted to Jesus first, and that their life lines up with the Bible. Find a role model in your life—not just one—but many, on many levels. You need to find a church where you can look up to the leadership as good role models. You need to have people around you with whom you can be joined together in friendship who will also be good role models to you. Do not merely spend time with people who live at a lower level than yours in the Christian life. Attach yourself to people who are ahead of you, so that they can bring you along with them. Jesus had His disciples following Him around everywhere. It was the same way with Paul and Timothy.

Paul tells us in 1 Corinthians 11:1, "Be ye followers of me, even as I also am of Christ."

The Doctor

One of my role models is the late D. Martyn Lloyd-Jones. Though he is dead, he lives on in his books. I can spend all the time I want to, sitting with "the Doctor." They called him that because he started into a medical career only to have God call him into the career of the ministry. He is one of my role models and I spend all kinds of time with "the Doctor." I love the way he opens up the Word of God and I thank God for the impact he has had upon my life.

There was a time when the Lord called G. Campbell Morgan to be a role model to D. Martyn Lloyd-Jones. Lloyd-Jones lived in Europe, but he was on a preaching tour here in America. One night, through the back door, came a lean, aging man. He recognized immediately that it was G. Campbell Morgan. After the message was over, Morgan came over to see "the Doctor" and said, "There was only one thing that could have drawn me here tonight, and that was that I knew you were preaching, and I came a long way to hear you." And then, getting very serious, he said, "I want to know if you will come and speak in my church at the end of the month. You'll have to come all the way back to Europe. I know it's short notice, but will you do it?" And Lloyd-Jones said, "Yes, I'll do it." Of course, he jumped at the chance; and as a result he ended up becoming Morgan's associate pastor. God knew that Morgan was to be the last role model that Lloyd-Jones needed before he went permanently on his own. When G. Campbell Morgan went to be with the Lord, Lloyd-Jones took over the church. Much of the great preaching that came forth is now preserved in his books that are sold all over the world.

Proven and Tried

Your service must follow on the heels of someone who is proven and tried, who has withstood the test of hard times and good times as well—people who, year after year, do not change. There are many people who one year preach one thing and the next year they preach another; and the following year they preach something else. Every year it's something different. My advice to you is: Do not follow that kind of a person. Follow someone who is consistently true to the Word.

SETTLING DOWN

As we begin to get established in our pattern of serving the Lord, it becomes crucial to allow the Lord to lead us to the geographical place He wants us to be in. Understanding this will bring great joy and save us from much unnecessary confusion and heartache.

The Lord would like to lead us in the paths of righteousness in terms of our settling down in the area, state, county, and even the actual house or apartment. Where you settle down should be something that is determined by being led in the paths of righteousness. Where you live should be prayerfully determined by where you go to church. The Lord wants to lead you in the paths of righteousness all the way down to the path to your own front door. So many Christians choose the place they are going to live for all the wrong reasons, often not even bothering to ask the Lord to lead them. They make their decision to go live under the "blue skies" somewhere just because they don't like where they currently live. This can cause major problems.

Lot's Downfall

This was Lot's downfall. The Bible tells us that Lot was a man who wanted blue skies. "And Lot lifted his eyes and saw all the plain of Jordan, that it was well watered everywhere... like the garden of the Lord, like the land of Egypt as you go toward Zoar. Then Lot chose for himself all the plain of Jordan, and Lot journeyed east.... Abram dwelt in the land of Canaan, and Lot dwelt in the cities of the plain and pitched his tent even as far as Sodom" (Genesis 13:10-12). Lot pitched his tent toward Sodom; that was his first mistake. His second mistake was that he moved into Sodom, and soon we find Lot taken captive. The man who freed him is the one who prayed about where he was living: Abraham. Lot's downfall came because he wanted the blue skies, the well-watered plain. He didn't want the problems of living a nomadic existence; and he ended up in trouble as he pitched his tent toward Sodom.

Over the years we've seen people make this mistake. They'll just charge off and move. But we've seen many of them come back. This is because they

97

didn't inquire counsel from the Lord as to where they were to live. I now counsel people to go find a church in the area they are planning on moving to *before* they find a house. This approach can save you months and even years of frustration! Every Christian should be tied into a local church; and where you choose to live should be related to where you worship.

SOCIAL INVOLVEMENTS

Another area that affects us is our social involvements. Who are your friends? We need to develop relationships with righteous people. Maybe they are not your role models, but they are people you spend time with; they are your friends, and they need to be godly people.

In 1 Corinthians 15:33 Paul makes a powerful statement: "Do not be deceived: 'Evil company corrupts good habits.'" We will become like those we associate with. Even if they seem to be very godly, there are people who love the Lord, but have become polluted with some kind of false doctrine. If you spend time with them, they will affect you. You've got to watch who your friends are, especially with regard to the old paths that you used to run on. Let the Lord lead you into righteous social involvements. Proverbs 1:15 says, "My son, do not walk in the way with them, keep your foot from their path."

Let the Lord Lead

Jesus needs to be the One who handles your social calendar. People, especially relatives, are going to ask you to do things that will conflict with what God is doing in your life.

One Thanksgiving we were invited to go out of town to visit some of our relatives. The pressure was incredible, and so we agreed to go. I realized that

I had not spent the quality time I needed to spend with my wife and family, yet I was saying "yes" to going out of town. Finally, I called up and told them that I could not go, explaining that I have some real priorities in my life and the Lord was telling me to take care of them. When I hung up the phone, my heart was flooded with peace. I went home and told Cindy, and her heart was also flooded with peace. We had a most wonderful Thanksgiving because we were right in the will of God. You must to learn to say "no." My first ministry is to my family. We have to take care of our primary needs first. Let Jesus have your social calendar and you'll have a lot more fun.

Where does the Lord lead us? The Lord will guide us in the paths of righteousness in our seeking, in our sanctification, in our service, in our settling down, and in our socializing.

With Jesus in the Valley of Death

Psalm 23: 4

Yea, though I walk through the valley of the shadow of death, I will fear no evil; For you are with me; Your rod and Your staff, they comfort me.

6

When I was twelve years old my grandfather died. At the time I was not a Christian. I will never forget the day of his funeral: the strange smell of so many flowers in one room, the weeping people, many of whom were dressed in black. All of this had a rather adverse effect upon my heart. But all of that was nothing compared to the emotional jolt I received as I walked up and peered over the edge into the open casket. I looked at what had been my grandfather—and I fell all to pieces. Why? Because death to me was a scary thing and I didn't know if he had ceased to exist. I didn't know if he was going to come back again for another time around in some kind of reincarnation. I didn't know if he was sleeping inside of that body forever. That was many years ago and, since then, I have come to know the truth about the valley of the shadow of death. It is my intention in this chapter to lay this truth before our hearts so that when our time comes we will be able to have an abundant entrance into the kingdom of God.

David says, "Yea, though I walk through the valley of the shadow of death..." There are some commentators who feel that David was not talking about death at all here, but simply about the hard times in life. However, it seems to me that he was talking about physical death because he goes on to speak of the goodness of the Lord in his life, and then of heaven. Though he was no doubt alluding to the hard times in life, he was also talking about the fact that God would be with him in death. And that is the blessed hope of the believer.

The people who do not know Jesus Christ don't want to think about death. People don't want to think about death because they are afraid of it. If you go to a funeral, watch the response of people as they go by the open casket. What you will see is the fear of the unknown.

Fearing the Unknown

Man does not like to think about death outside of Jesus Christ because it's frightening. We are talking about going from the known to the unknown, from all of our relationships to maybe no relationships at all. Those who are outside of Jesus Christ don't know what's happening on the other side of death. The Bible says in Hebrews 2:15 that Jesus came to "release those who through fear of death were all their lifetime subject to bondage."

Every person living and breathing today on this planet has a fear of death. I can remember being very small, lying in bed at night and thinking about dying. I would cry sometimes while lying on my pillow because it was so unnerving. The Bible tells us that from the time we are little until the time we are old we are held in the bondage of the fear of death. And yet, for the Christian, death is not something to fear.

Paul wrote to the Philippians, "For I am hard pressed between the two, having a desire to depart and be with Christ, which is far better. Nevertheless to remain in the flesh is more needful for you" (Philippians 1:23-24). It was not that Paul wanted to leave this earth as a result of being unable to cope, because he had a wonderful life in spite of all the persecution. He said, "For me to live is Christ..." (Philippians 1:21). However, he knew there was something better than this life; and that waiting for him was a promise of being with Jesus Christ. It is evident in the way Paul ministered that he had no fear of death. He lived constantly under the threat of death, but it didn't hold him back because he was a Christian and he knew the hope of eternal life in Jesus.

I want to divide this chapter into three sections: First, the problem of death; second, the presentation of life that we find in Jesus Christ in His resurrection; and third, the presence of Jesus with us in death.

THE PROBLEM OF DEATH

First we will examine the problems that surround the whole idea of death. David says, "Yea, though I walk through the valley of the shadow of death..." Every one of us is pointed right now toward death; and we are steadily moving in that direction. And even with all of man's advances in technology, it seems that life on planet earth has only become more uncertain.

One day a man walked into our church and sat down for the service. He did not know Jesus Christ. That Sunday he walked out of church and got on an airplane bound for the East Coast. But the jet crashed just outside of Detroit and that man died. We never know when we are going to go. The truth is that we are only a heartbeat away from eternity. We must come to grips with the whole idea of death so that we might be ready for it.

Consider the Lies

Let's begin by considering the lies about death that keep people from coming to rest solely in Jesus Christ for their salvation. If we are going to be ready to face death, then we must consider the lies that the devil has propagated to deceive people into not being ready for death—not knowing Jesus Christ when that hour comes.

One of the greatest deceptions the devil has spawned on mankind is the lie of purgatory. The

Roman Catholic church teaches that there is a place called "Purgatory." They teach that it is a place where you can have a "second chance" after you die.

That's a lie; that is a damnable heresy. You might be thinking, "How can you say that? What a strong, unloving statement!" Strong? Unloving? There is not one statement in the entire Word of God about a purgatory! Jesus said very clearly, "No man comes to the Father but by Me!" How many people do you think are in hell right now who were told that there was going to be a purgatory where they could clean up their mistakes and go on into heaven? To me, the lie of purgatory is the unloving thing. The most loving thing is to tell people the truth. Purgatory is a damnable heresy spawned by the devil that has sent millions of people down the broad road to destruction, all the while letting them think they were on the road to eternal life!

Reincarnation

Another big lie (popular with Eastern religions) is reincarnation. Reincarnation basically teaches that if you do not live up to expectations in this life, you will have another chance when you come back in a next life. Reincarnation is another lie of the devil to draw you away from the truth of being accountable to God in Jesus Christ.

Lighted Tunnel

Beyond reincarnation and purgatory, there is a new one. I call it the lie of the "lighted tunnel with the friends holding flowers in the field at the end." According to this notion, after death you have an out-of-body experience where you wander down a tunnel. You will find friends reaching out their hands, telling you how beautiful and peaceful things are. They will take you out into a field of flowers and tell you, "Everything is wonderful here..." And then a voice comes out of somewhere and says, "You can't stay; you have to go back!" And so they come back into this life to write a book and tell how they saw a light in a tunnel and friends in a field. And they sum it all up by saying that no matter who we are or how we live, we all get to go to that great place of light and love. That is a lie of the devil. The Bible tells us in 2 Corinthians 11:14 that Satan has the ability to transform himself into an angel of light.

Now, I don't know exactly what happens when you die and where you're going after that. There may be a tunnel with some light; I don't know. But I do know one thing: for the most part, this doctrine is a lie and there are many people who have bought into it. They think it doesn't matter how they live because they are going to a wonderful place with their friends. I can't imagine how frightening it will be when those people wake up on the other side and there's no field, no flowers, and their friends aren't waiting for them.

Soul Sleep

Another view that has been very popular throughout the cults and even in the church is that people will sleep in the grave. The Bible says in Hebrews 9:27, "And as it is appointed for men to die once, but after this the judgment." That contradicts the idea of purgatory, reincarnation, soul sleep, and the lighted tunnel. After death, people are going to stand before God and give an account for what they did with Jesus Christ. That is the truth that will send you to heaven forever. And all of those other things are lies. If we are going to be ready for death, we must first consider the lies.

Contemplate the Truth

Every person, Christian or not, should stop and contemplate the serious truth of what is really going to happen at death. The Bible says, "Then I saw a great white throne and Him who sat on it, from whose face the earth and the heaven fled away. And there was found no place for them. And I saw the dead, small and great, standing before God, and books were opened. And another book was opened which is the Book of Life. And the dead were judged according to their works, by the things which were written in the books. The sea gave up the dead who were in it, and Death and Hades delivered up the dead who were in them. And they were judged, each one according to his works. Then Death and Hades were cast into the lake of fire. This is the second death. And anyone not found written in the Book of Life was cast into the lake of fire" (Revelation 20: 11-15).

If you don't know Jesus Christ, you need to contemplate that truth, or you will not be ready when God comes in your final hour.

For those who do know Christ, death is a beautiful thing—a contrast to being thrown into the lake of fire. The Lord presents this alternative: "And I saw a new heaven and a new earth, for the first heaven and the first earth had passed away. Also there was no more sea. Then I, John, saw the holy city, New Jerusalem, coming down out of heaven from God, prepared as a bride adorned for her husband. And I heard a loud voice from heaven saying, 'Behold, the tabernacle of God is with men, and He will dwell with them, and they shall be His people, and God Himself will be with them and be their God. And God will wipe away every tear from their eyes; there shall be no more death, nor sorrow, nor crying; and there shall be no more pain, for the former things have passed away.' Then He who sat on the throne said, 'Behold, I make all things new.' And He said to me, 'Write, for these words are

108

true and faithful.' And He said to me, 'It is done! I am the Alpha and the Omega, the Beginning and the End. I will give of the fountain of the water of life freely to him who thirsts' " (Revelation 21:1-6).

Calculate the Changes

It's not enough to contemplate the truth. It is not enough just to believe that there is a heaven and a hell. You need to calculate the changes you must make.

If you're going to be ready for death, you need to calculate the necessary changes. You need to review your life honestly, looking at where you have been, where you are going, what your plans are, and what you are doing with Jesus today.

The psalmist says, "So teach us to number our days, that we may gain a heart of wisdom" (Psalm 90:12). We are told that death is to be a tutor to us; to look to the end, to number our days, and then to apply our hearts to wisdom that we might walk in the things of God in this brief life that we have. If we are to believe and to be ready, we need to begin to live in the reality that this life is going to come to an end.

That's the problem with most young people; they think that they are going to live forever. We need to live in the knowledge that there will be an end to all of this. We need to live in the certainty that we will stand before God soon and we will have to give an account for the things in this life.

Great Examples

I love what David Brainerd, that great saint of God and missionary to the Indians, said in his diary, "I long to be a flame of fire continually glowing in the divine service, and building up Christ's kingdom to my last and dying breath." He died when he was only twenty-nine years old.

Jonathan Edwards, another wonderful man of God who brought renewal to this country, said of David Brainerd: "His example in victorious death had its impact upon my entire family. The man was such a great saint of God. But he lived as though it was going to end some day. I am going to live in such a way that I am a bright burning fire for the Lord right up to the end."

Jim Elliot was a modern-day martyr. One of his most often quoted sayings is that "It is no sacrifice to give up that which you cannot keep for that which you cannot lose." Those are great words.

We need to begin to live our lives with a view toward the end, numbering our days that we may be ready when our time comes. Remember: It's no sacrifice to give up now what you cannot keep for that which you cannot lose. One day, an Auca Indian in South America threw a spear, and Jim Elliot went home to be with Jesus at the age of thirty-three.

It seems that some people refuse to stop to contemplate the truth and consider the lies. Sometimes the Lord will step in and will give certain people a taste of death.

A Second Chance

I remember talking to a man whom I worked with years ago. He began to tell me about his marital problems and his drug abuse. Then he told me the story of what I perceived to be his second chance: "One night while we were partying in a Volkswagon van, we ended up racing down the freeway and the van ended up piling into a semi-truck. My two friends in the front seat were killed instantly. I was asleep in the back and was suddenly awakened as my whole body was thrown forward and smashed right into the seats behind the people who were killed. I should have died also; but somehow I lived."

I sat there and I asked God what I should tell this man. I told him that God gave him a second chance. How was it that he lived? How did he survive the impact of the semi-truck to get up and walk away alive? God gave him a taste of death that he might get serious and sober and look to the end and begin to live his life in the awareness that one of these days God will call him into account.

The beautiful thing is that man came to Christ. I said, "You've been given a second chance and you're not taking advantage of it. Your wife is divorcing you, you have been a horrible man, and you are rebelling against God." He began to weep and he gave his life to Jesus Christ. God sometimes gives us a second chance, but if you refuse to respond, He may bring you to the point where you're close to death.

There are many Christians living on the outer edge as well. They are on their way to heaven, but God says He gives us a talent and wants a full return on it, so that we can have an abundant entrance into His kingdom. Sometimes the Lord will bring Christians as well to the place where it's too close for comfort. He has sometimes given them a taste of death too if they have refused to contemplate these things we are talking about.

Do you want to go too close for comfort? Wouldn't you rather just simply say, "Lord, take it all! I am going the easy way. Guide me; and I'll follow wherever You take me."

We are told in Ecclesiastes 7:2 and 4: "It is better to go to the house of mourning than to go to the house of feasting, for that is the end of all men; and the living will take it to heart.... The heart of the wise is in the house of mourning, but the heart of fools is in the house of mirth."

God intends that we would be ready so that death would not take us by surprise. It is imperative that we consider the lies and then go on to contemplate the truth. Then we need to go beyond that and

111

calculate all the changes that we need to make in our lives today.

The Dream House

My wife, Cindy, was working a number of years ago at a hospital in a unit where many people were dying. She had a chance to visit with a man who had leukemia. Here was a man who was near death with an incurable disease. He began to tell her his life story. He and his wife had saved all of their money to come out to California and buy their dream house in Newport Beach. He was hoping to get out of the hospital alive and go home and settle down with his wife and enjoy their dream house. But Cindy knew that he was going to die. She knew that there would be no dream house for this man. She said to him, "You have leukemia." And she began to tell him: "You're going to die. The chances of your seeing that dream house are very slim. You need to consider that there are a lot of lies about death these days." She went through the lies with him, and then she began telling him that he needed to contemplate the truth. She witnessed to him the good news of Jesus Christ and told him about heaven and hell. She told him that he needed to contemplate where he was in respect to this. "You need to think about the changes that are necessary right now to get you ready to go." She told him that he had a dream house in heaven *if* he would ask Jesus into his heart. She went on to say, "For two thousand years, He has been working on the dwelling places in the Father's house where those who believe in Him will live forever. Now that is a dream house!" She told him that it was as simple as going back to his room and getting down on his knees and asking Jesus to forgive him for his sin, come into his heart, and take over his life. As they parted, she strongly encouraged him to do just that.

112

He went back to his room and the following day he was up very early. At six o'clock in the morning, the nurses found him kneeling beside his bed, praying. They came back at seven and he was still praying. They came back at seven-thirty, and on he prayed. They came back at eight and he had gone to be in his dream house: the one that Jesus had built for him.

That's the goodness of God. The Lord gave him his chance and he believed. He considered the lies, he was willing to go on to contemplate the truth, and he calculated what needed to be done to be ready.

THE PRESENTATION OF LIFE

Having looked at the problem of death, let's look at the presentation of life.

Jesus shows us the way though the valley of death in His resurrection. We are told in Hebrews 2:14-15: "Inasmuch then as the children have partaken of flesh and blood, He Himself likewise shared in the same, that though death He might destroy him who had the power of death, that is, the devil, and release those who through fear of death were all their lifetime subject to bondage." Jesus came to destroy death. In 2 Timothy 1:10 Paul writes, "...but has now been revealed by the appearing of our Savior Jesus Christ, who has abolished death and brought life and im-mortality to light through the gospel..." Jesus has abolished death and brought life and immortality to light through the gospel. The word "abolished" is the Greek word *kartargeo.* It means "to be made of no effect." When Jesus abolished death, He made it of no effect. The idea is that He has emptied death of all that which fills the heart with fear. Jesus, in His sacrifice for our sins and in His resurrection, has emptied death of all that filled our hearts as Chris-tians with fear.

The Lord was very careful to demonstrate clearly that He truly had abolished death, and that He had

113

taken the fear out of it. He gave a full presentation of what happens after you die.

Acts 1:3 tells us that Jesus "...presented Himself alive after His suffering by many infallible proofs, being seen by them during forty days and speaking of the things pertaining to the kingdom of God." Jesus, after He rose from the dead, was so concerned about taking the fear out of death for His people that He stayed around for forty days to show us what happens after death. He gave us a full presentation of the resurrected life.

For forty days, Jesus built a bridge of infallible proofs, the Bible tells us, so that He might show us the way through and take the fear out of death for those who believe upon Him.

Revelation

The first infallible proof is the revelation of the fact that there is actually life after death. Mary came from the tomb of Jesus, weeping. "But Mary stood outside by the tomb weeping, and as she wept she stooped down and looked into the tomb. And she saw two angels in white sitting, one at the head and the other at the feet, where the body of Jesus had lain. Then they said to her, 'Woman, why are you weeping?' She said to them, 'Because they have taken away my Lord, and I do not know where they have laid Him.' Now when she had said this, she turned around and saw Jesus standing there, and did not know that it was Jesus. Jesus said to her, 'Woman, why are you weeping? Whom are you seeking?' She, supposing Him to be the gardener, said to Him, 'Sir, if You have carried Him away, tell me where You have laid Him, and I will take Him away.' Jesus said to her, 'Mary!' She turned and said to Him 'Rabboni!' (which is to say, Teacher). Jesus said to her, 'Do not cling to Me, for I have not yet ascended to My Father; but go to My brethren and say to them, 'I am ascending to My Father and your Father, and to My God and your God'" (John 20: 11-17).

Jesus is living proof that there is life after death.

Presentation

In the Gospel of Luke, Jesus gives us a presentation of the kind of body that you will have after you have been raised from the dead. Jesus said, "'Behold My hands and My feet, that it is I Myself. Handle Me and see, for a spirit does not have flesh and bones as you see I have.' When He had said this, He showed them His hands and His feet. But while they still did not believe for joy, and marveled, He said to them, 'Have you any food here?' They gave Him a piece of a broiled fish and some honeycomb. And He took it and ate in their presence" (Luke 24:39-43).

Jesus wants us to know that our resurrection bodies will be similar to our earthly bodies.

Demonstration

And then He went another step beyond that: He gave them a revelation; He gave them a presentation; and then he went on to give them a demonstration.

Have you ever wondered what kind of a body you'll have? Will you be a spirit floating on a white cloud with a harp throughout eternity? Jesus wants you to know that you will be yourself, and that you'll have a body. He wants you to see the nature of it. The Bible says: "Then, the same day at evening, being the first day of the week, when the doors were shut where the disciples were assembled, for fear of the Jews, Jesus came and stood in the midst, and said to them, 'Peace be with you'" (John 20:19).

The disciples were in a place with the door shut when Jesus walked through the wall and appeared in the middle of the room.

115

And then, just to reinforce it: "And after eight days His disciples were again inside, and Thomas with them. Jesus came, the doors being shut, and stood in the midst, and said, 'Peace to you!'" (John 20:26). Jesus wants us to know what our new bodies will be like: They will be glorified bodies; they are not going to be anything like these old bodies that we are carrying around right now.

Jesus kept going back and forth from the unknown to the known. They were in the room with the doors locked and they didn't know where He was. He appears! Out of the unknown comes the known. It's Jesus again; the form of the body is the same, but it is a different body. He is building a bridge of infallible proofs to show us what it is going to be like on the other side of the grave. Thus, we are not afraid to die because we know where we are going, and we know what it's going to be like, and how good it's going to be.

Emmaus Road

On the Emmaus road, Jesus appeared to two disciples. "Now it came to pass, as He sat at the table with them, that He took bread, blessed and broke it, and gave it to them. Then their eyes were opened and they knew Him; and He vanished from their sight" (Luke 24:30-31). His glorified body demonstrated His ability to go from the known to the unknown.

He wants to cover every side of the truth so that there is no fear left in our hearts. And the explanation in Acts 1:3 says, "...during forty days [He kept] speaking of the things pertaining to the kingdom of God."

Jesus wants us to know that there is no reason to fear going to be with Him; He takes our fear of death. The Bible tells us in Luke 24:32, "And they said to one another, 'Did not our heart burn within us while He talked with us on the road, and while He opened the Scriptures to us?'" They did not know where Jesus went and they were full of the fear of death when suddenly their hearts started burning as He opened up the Scriptures. They began to burn with a desire to go to the place He was telling them about. He filled their hearts with a burning desire to go to heaven.

He gave them a thorough presentation of the resurrected life by taking the sting out of death. It reminds me of an account that I came across while reading about Charles Spurgeon.

Gone to Heaven!

Spurgeon was preaching on a hot summer afternoon on the joys of heaven. "And there was a woman's eye that especially caught mine. I knew not why it was, but it seemed to fascinate me. And as I spoke of heaven, she seemed to drink in every word, and her eyes flashed back again the thoughts I uttered. She seemed to lead me on to speak more and more of the streets of gold and the gates of pearl, till suddenly her eyes appeared to me to be too fixed. At last it struck me that, while I had been talking of heaven, she had gone there.

"I paused and asked if someone in the pew would kindly see whether the friend sitting there was not dead, and in a moment her husband said, 'She is dead, sir.' I had known her long as a consistent Christian, and as I stood there, I half wished that I could have changed places with her. There was not a sigh, nor a tear. She seemed to drink in the thoughts of heaven, and then immediately go to enjoy it" (Tom Carter, *Spurgeon At His Best*, Grand Rapids: Baker Book House, 1989, p. 53). What a way to go!

The Christian has the joy of living life on the foundational truth that Jesus has taken the sting out of death for us.

THE PRESENCE OF JESUS

The third very encouraging truth is that His presence will be with us at death. On the night before His death, Jesus was trying to comfort His disciples. A few hours before His death He told them, "In My Father's house are many mansions; if it were not so, I would have told you..." (John 14:2). He was preparing them for the fact that He was going to leave and then, some day, they were going to leave also. And He said: "'I go to prepare a place for you. And if I go and prepare a place for you, I will come again and receive you to Myself; that where I am, there you may be also. And where I go you know, and the way you know.' Thomas said to Him, 'Lord, we do not know where You are going, and how can we know the way?' Jesus said to him, 'I am the way, the truth, and the life. No one comes to the Father except through Me.'" He went on to say, "I will not leave you orphans; I will come to you. A little while longer and the world will see Me no more, but you will see Me. Because I live, you will live also" (John 14:2-6, 18-19).

We wonder how we will be in the hour of death. Jesus has promised that during the hour of death He will never leave us nor forsake us; He will come personally to take us to the Father.

Isn't that a comfort? He later proved this with the martyr, Stephen.

Stephen

The mob was about to kill Stephen when his face began to glow. He looked and he said, "Look! I see the heavens opened and the Son of Man standing..." (Acts 7:56). The Bible says that after His ascension into heaven Jesus sat down at the right hand of the Father. We see Him here—standing—because He knew Stephen was coming. He stood up to receive Stephen. Stephen was under full control because Jesus had come to take him home. And so he was able to forgive those who were killing him.

Our Coronation Day

The death of Dwight L. Moody is another case in point. He was a great man of God, living every day as though he were ready to go. A few hours before finishing his course in this life, Dwight L. Moody is said to have caught a glimpse of the glory awaiting him. Awakening from a sleep, he said: "Earth recedes, Heaven opens before me. If this is death, it is sweet. There is no valley here. God is calling me, and I must go." His son, who was standing by his bedside, said, "No, no, Father, you are dreaming."

"No," said Mr. Moody, "I am not dreaming: I have been within the gates: I have seen the children's faces." A short time elapsed and then, following what seemed to the family to be the death struggle of his physical body, he spoke again: "This is my triumph; this my coronation day. It is glorious." And then he went to be with Jesus.

The Bible tells us that to be absent from the body is to be present with the Lord (2 Corinthians 5:8). As people who have been born again through faith in the Lord Jesus Christ, we do not need to fear death because Jesus will be with us. It will be our coronation day; it will be the end of our race—it will be our entrance into glory forever!

Anointed
and
Overflowing

Psalm 23:5

You prepare a table
before me
in the presence
of my enemies;
You anoint my head
with oil; My cup
runs over.

7

Have you ever thought about what an incredible thing it is to be a Christian and to be blessed to the point of overflowing in the midst of such a dark world? We read in the papers about the constant threat of war. The media around us are continually seeking to seduce us with the lust of the flesh. The philosophies of man are constantly pounding in our ears, pulling us toward the pride of life. The devil, head of all fallen principalities and powers of the darkness of this world, is always going about as a roaring lion seeking whom he may devour. His demons are constantly tempting, oppressing, deceiving, and attacking us. Yet, in the midst of all this, we as Christians somehow have the privilege of what Jesus Christ calls "life...and that more abundantly." How can all of this happen the way it does? David gives us the only possible answer when he says, "You prepare a table before me in the presence of my enemies; You anoint my head with oil; You make my cup to overflow."

The statement that he makes encompasses everything that he has said to this point in Psalm Twenty-three.

THE TABLE PREPARED

The Christian life is a battle from the start to the finish. Paul said concerning his life, "without and within are fightings" (2 Corinthians 7:5). It seems that when there is rest in our own hearts in the eye of the storm, there are storms going on around us—

either outside attacks from the enemy or attacks on the lives of the people around us. There is always conflict in the Christian life. We find that out very quickly as we come to know Jesus and walk with Him.

If it were not for God preparing a table of blessing in the midst of our enemies, there would be very few blessings at all, because there are enemies constantly surrounding us.

Even in the midst of the constant battles around David, the Lord had been faithful in his life to bless him and meet his needs to the point of overflowing. What a powerful lesson this is to learn. This is the essence of what Paul tells us in the New Testament, that "even when we don't believe, He abides faithful." Year in and year out, the Lord is constantly preparing a table of blessing in the midst of any and all circumstances of life.

The Sheep's Enemies

In the country where David was living, during the summertime they would lead the sheep up onto a higher ground to the greener pastures. Many countries call this the "table land." "Mesa" is the Spanish word for "table" and is their name for the flat lands of the higher mountains. There the shepherd would take his sheep each summer, up onto the higher mountains to find that good grazing land. Here, he would literally have to prepare the table, the flat land, for the sheep to be able to feed safely.

As we learned in an earlier chapter, sheep are dependent on the shepherd's protection, being defenseless of themselves. As they would come to the various grazing lands in that part of the world, they had a number of different problems. One was a little snake called an adder. These adders had a way of coming up out of their holes when the sheep would come into the grazing land.

The adders had little holes that they lived in down in the ground. When the sheep would come by, the snakes would dart out of their holes and bite the sheep right on their noses. Sometimes the bite could be so severe that it could poison a sheep and kill him. To counteract this, the good shepherd would meticulously take a very thick oil or grease and rub it all around the opening of each hole where the snake could come out. The sheep would come in and begin to graze after the shepherd had very carefully prepared all of that pasture. The adders would come darting out of their holes—but the oil would cause them to flop around and back down inside again. They would become captives within their own little houses. The sheep would then be safe. That was one way of preparing the table in the midst of enemies.

Weeds

Another problem was poisonous weeds. The shepherd would often have to get down on his hands and knees, with any helpers that he had, and go through the entire pasture, pulling up the poisonous weeds which could harm and even kill the sheep.

There were other things the good shepherd had to do, including constantly watching to defend the sheep against the cougars and wolves which would come to attack the defenseless sheep. The best feeding is done right in the midst of many enemies, and it is all made possible by the work, care, and protection of the shepherd.

The Promised Blessing

The concept of the Lord preparing a table before us in the midst of our enemies is almost exactly parallel to what we have just looked at. As we look in the

Bible we see a picture of this whole process. As the Lord led the people of Israel out of Egypt, He promised them that they would have a good land, a land flowing with milk and honey.

The idea of a land flowing with milk and honey speaks of a lush, fertile agricultural land. When the spies went in from the outside, they came back with such a large cluster of grapes that they carried it on a pole between two of them. That was just one indication of the blessedness of the land.

Enemies

It was truly an abundant land and a blessed land, but we find that this blessed promised land was a land filled with enemies. That is a beautiful picture of what David is talking about. God had prepared a lush, rich table for his people right in the midst of their enemies.

We find them coming in, spying out the land, then returning and showing the good things from the land. But only two men were filled with enough faith to see the table God had prepared in the midst of their enemies: Joshua and Caleb. The rest of the spies said that there were giants in the land who made men look like grasshoppers in comparison, as well as massive, high-walled cities. After hearing the report of these spies, the people soon lost all hope of ever going on to conquer these enemies; thus their visions of enjoying the blessedness of the land the Lord had promised were quickly shattered.

God had a plan all worked out in which He was going to fully enable them to conquer their enemies and partake of all the blessedness this great land had to offer. Yet, in their hasty, rebellious unbelief, they refused to take God at his Word. So God let them wander in the wilderness for forty years until all

126

who carried that unbelief in their hearts had died. Only Joshua and Caleb survived their generation.

Following His Plan

After many years of wandering in the wilderness and missing out on all the blessings God had prepared for them in the promised land, the Lord called them to enter. As they passed over the River Jordan, the first thing they encountered was a "city walled up to heaven."

Here is a truth we must guard in our hearts for all of our Christian life: When God calls us to His table in the midst of our enemies, He always has a way of enabling us to overcome them. This is the foundational principle on which Jesus Christ gives His promise of the abundant life!

Next, we see Joshua on a hillside overlooking the entire scene and the Angel of the Lord appears to him as he is praying. Many commentators feel that this Angel of the Lord may have been Jesus Christ Himself appearing in what is called a "theophany": Jesus appearing in the Old Testament to His people before His incarnation. This Angel of the Lord appears to Joshua and tells him that the Lord will fight the battle.

I find it fascinating that God gave Joshua the detailed plan of how to conquer Jericho—and how perfectly it worked. They marched once around the city for six days. The seventh day they marched around seven times and shouted for the glory of God. The power of God fell, and so did the walls which were keeping them from getting to the blessed land. They went into the land and began to partake of its blessings. From that time, as long as they sought the Lord and followed His plan, they were able to enjoy the blessing of God.

We learn from this that there is a "good land" prepared by God, a land of milk and honey. It is a land in the midst of enemies, but God has a way of enabling us to get past all of the enemies' strongholds to inherit the blessedness that He has for us. The key to Joshua's being able to follow the Lord's plan was his faith. This is the lesson the apostle John learned from our Lord and recorded in his first Epistle, "And this is the victory that has overcome the world—our faith" (1 John 5:4).

TODAY

The Bible says in 1 John 5:19, "We know that we are of God, and the whole world lies under the sway of the wicked one." The Bible tells us that the entire world is in wickedness. These are among the most wicked times in the history of the world, and yet the Word of God tells us that the Lord has prepared a table for us in the midst of our enemies.

What an incredible thing it is that we now sit at the Lord's table when we used to sit at the devil's table. In 1 Peter 4:2-4, Peter writes: "...that he no longer should live the rest of his time in the flesh for the lusts of men, but for the will of God. For we have spent enough of our past lifetime in doing the will of the Gentiles—when we walked in licentiousness, lusts, drunkenness, revelries, drinking parties, and abominable idolatries. In regard to these, they think it strange that you do not run with them in the same flood of dissipation, speaking evil of you."

When a person becomes a Christian, our old friends look at our lives and wonder what happened. "Why don't you go that way with us any more? Why don't you do these things with us?" The reason we don't is because of what the Bible tells us in the Song of Solomon: "He brought me to the banqueting house, and his banner over me was love" (Song of Solomon 2:4). We are sitting at the Lord's table now, and when we begin to fill ourselves up with the things of His table, our appetite for the things of the world goes away. That is an issue which is impossible for non-Christians to understand. They are always wondering why they have such a great magnetism toward the things of the world, and we do not. The truth is that they continue to hunger for those empty things because they are not feasting at the satisfying table of the Lord.

Blessings

What are some of the blessings God has for us at His table? One of the greatest is the unspeakable joy He places in our hearts. Proverbs 15:15 says, "All the days of the afflicted are evil, but he who is of a merry heart has a continual feast."

This joy is especially full as we gather with the saints to worship our Lord. When you have God's people dwelling together in unity and simplicity, feasting on His Word, you have a people that have a continual feast.

Coming to the table of the Lord in the midst of your enemies could be something intensely practical. It could be coming to the Lord's table to remember Him in communion; it could be something like finding a church where the worship and the teaching are richly anointed by the Holy Spirit. To me, that is one of the greatest blessings in all of life. It reminds me of the situation the people were facing in Jesus' day. Their religious leaders, as religious as they were, were so unbelievably carnal and evil that Jesus went as far as to call them "children of the devil." Yet in the midst of this, we see multitudes of the common people coming to hear Him gladly, feeding on the bread of heaven. That is the way we feel when we find a good, blessed church in the midst of a generation of cold, lukewarm, and often apostate church leaders.

Your Bible

Ultimately, the Lord's table in the midst of your enemies will be your Bible. In Deuteronomy 8:3, Moses wrote: "...He humbled you, allowed you to hunger, and fed you with manna which you did not know nor did your fathers know, that He might make you know that man shall not live by bread alone; but man lives by every word that proceeds from the mouth of the Lord."

The lesson of the manna is that we don't live by physical bread alone. We live by the words of God and by the bread that comes from heaven. The Word of God is our feast.

In my life, the most dramatic changes have been made as a result of the Word of God. For a long time, I neglected my Bible and let it get dusty. As time went by, I could not figure out why I was so unhappy, with so little victory and joy as a Christian. Then I discovered Job's secret: "I have not departed from the commandment of His lips; I have treasured the words of His mouth more than my necessary food" (Job 23:12). How could a man go through the loss of everything he owned and loved, and respond on his knees in worship the way Job did? People see the trials that Job went through and they fail to realize that the powerful message of Job's life was his deep love for the Word of God; and, as a result of that, his great grasp on the sovereignty of God and his understanding of the goodness of God. When he lost everything, he fell to his knees and said, "The Lord gave, and the Lord has taken away; blessed be the name of the Lord" (Job 1:21). Behind that behavior was a soul anchored in, and well fed on, the Word of God.

If we would have the same hunger and thirst for the Word, we would find the power and the belief that Job had; and we would also find the blessings that he received at the table of the Lord.

Scripture says: "Ho, everyone that thirsteth, come ye to the waters, and he that no money; come ye, buy, and eat; yea, come, buy wine and milk without money and without price. Wherefore do ye spend money for that which is not bread? And your labour for that which satisfieth not? Hearken diligently unto me, and eat ye that which is good, and let your soul delight itself in fatness" (Isaiah 55:1-2, King James Version).

If you want a fat *soul*, the only way to get it is in feasting on the Word of God.

A Hungry Pastor

I love the story a pastor shared at a conference I attended. This particular brother has an incredible love for God's Word. He had gotten extremely busy in his life with conferences that week: teaching, ministering to the men, and so on. Finally, he slipped away into his office where he hadn't been in a couple of days. As soon as he got in there, he shut the door and locked it. He then picked up his Bible and he held it to his chest as he backed into the corner, saying, "God, as much as I love the work You have called me to, I have gotten so busy this week, it has all been taking me away from You and my time alone in Your Word! I've got to be alone with You—I've got to get back to Your Word!"

It speaks to me so much that this man who is being greatly used for the Lord has his primary focus on God and his time alone with Him. He realizes how essential it is to sit at the Lord's table to be fed from His Word.

I realize that the feasting at the table in the midst of the enemies is going to be done at my Bible. Jesus wants to take our hearts and impress everything in the Bible all over them until we begin to live within the pages of His Book. As Charles

131

Spurgeon once said, "You ought to be so saturated with the word of God that if somebody cut you, you would bleed 'biblene.'"

THE ANOINTING GIVEN

In order to enjoy the table which God has set for us, there must be an anointing. God has more than accommodated us in the middle of our enemies with all of the good things that we have been talking about. David goes on to say, "He anoints my head with oil." This is the anointing God gives us for blessings. The table is out there and God has it prepared, but we will never get to those blessings on our own strength.

When David says, "He anoints my head with oil," he is speaking of the work of the Holy Spirit and the blessing of God upon our lives. David was very much aware of the anointing of the Holy Spirit upon his life.

We need a fresh anointing of God every day of our lives to keep us protected from the sin around us. Then we become like a greased pig at the fair when the devil comes chasing after us. When we are walking in the anointing of the Holy Spirit, sin can't get its grip on us. If we begin to harden our hearts to the Lord and turn from Him and quench the Holy Spirit, we will become like glue, inviting sin to stick to us.

In Isaiah 61:3, Isaiah says that the Lord has come "To console those who mourn in Zion, to give them beauty for ashes, the oil of joy for mourning, the garment of praise for the spirit of heaviness; that they may be called trees of righteousness, the planting of the Lord, that He may be glorified."

In Luke 11:13, Jesus says, "If you then, being evil, know how to give good gifts to your children, how much more will your heavenly Father give the Holy Spirit to those who ask Him!"

We are told by the Lord Jesus to ask for the Holy Spirit in order that the Holy Spirit can bring us to a place of blessedness. He is our Divine Escort; and we will never get there without Him. The walls of Jericho never would have fallen if God had not given Joshua a divine plan. The power of His Spirit which created the heavens and the universe knocked those walls down. It's the same way in our lives.

The anointing of the Holy Spirit enables us to enjoy the blessings that God has for us. The Lord is able to come to us in the midst of the battle when we are at our lowest point. The Holy Spirit has a way of coming to us and renewing our hearts in a wonderful and marvelous way.

THE OVERFLOWING CUP

When we are feasting at the table the Lord has prepared for us and walking under the anointing of the Holy Spirit, we eventually get so blessed and so full that we can say with David: "My cup overflows."

The Word of God tells us that if we will sow in righteousness, we will reap in mercy. "Break up your fallow ground, for it is time to seek the Lord, till he comes and rains righteousness on you" (Hosea 10:12). The overflowing cup is directly tied into sowing to the Spirit.

We are told in Psalm 126:5, "Those who sow in tears shall reap in joy."

It's a matter of choices. Some people feel that their problems are so big that they will never have a cup that is full. Yet God completely understands our problems and He has not called any Christian to a half-filled cup.

Uzziah was sixteen years old when he became king. The Bible says that as long as he sought the Lord, God caused him to prosper and He blessed him. Uzziah had everything, feasting at the "table of God"; but he made a decision to go into the temple

133

and offer the sacrifice and exalt himself in pride. The priests came in and tried to argue with him, telling him to stop. But he refused and God struck him with leprosy, and he remained a leper until the day of his death (2 Chronicles 26:16-21).

The choice to serve God brought the prosperity of God and His blessedness upon his life, and then the choice to rebel in pride took the blessing away.

We, like Uzziah, will be blessed as long as we seek the Lord. We will feast at the table of the Lord and have the anointing of the Lord and our cups will overflow. It is a choice that no one else can make for us.

The God We Serve

Biblical scholar Haddon Robinson said: "This is the God we serve... this is the blessing He brings... with Him the calf is always the fatted calf; the robe is always the best robe; the joy is always unspeakable; and the peace always passes understanding. There is no grudging in God's goodness. He does not measure His goodness by drops like a druggist filling a prescription. It comes to us in floods. If we only recognized the lavish abundance of His gifts, what a difference it would make in our lives! If every meal were taken as a gift from His hand, it would be almost a sacrament" (Haddon W. Robinson, *The Good Shepherd*, Chicago: Moody Press, 1968, p. 52).

May God give us a fresh illumination in our hearts to know that He has called every one of us to an overflowing cup, that we have a table in the middle of our enemies, and we have an anointing from God if we will only trust Him.

Heaven

Psalm 23:6

Surely goodness and
mercy
shall follow me
All the days of my life;
And I will dwell in the
house of the Lord
forever.

8

David writes, "Surely goodness and mercy shall follow me all the days of my life; and I will dwell in the house of the Lord forever." He says in another Psalm, "One thing have I desired of the Lord, that I will seek: That I may dwell in the house of the Lord all the days of my life, to behold the beauty of the Lord..." (Psalm 27:4).

The deep desire of David's heart was to be with God forever. David had a wonderful relationship with God during his life, and out of that intimacy came the longing for heaven.

I talk to people who tell me about the hope we have of eternal life, heaven, and future glory. When someone says that this hope does not help them in their trials now, they are only telling me that they are not intimate with God. If you find yourself at this point not under the hope and the power of the glory of heaven, it is probably either because you have never really had it or because the cares of this life have crowded it out. Either way, it is the intent of this study to place that living hope at the forefront of your mind and heart in a lasting way.

The hope of heaven, when it burns brightly in your heart, has a way of overriding all of the problems and circumstances of your life. Our problems are just as bad as those of the people in the world—the difference is that the Christian has a bright hope burning in his heart. When that hope is genuine, it has a way of causing you to look around at your problems and realize that these are

137

light afflictions in relationship to the glory that is to come. The hope of heaven should have a very real effect upon your life.

There is much emphasis today on "me," "self," and "right now." This preoccupation with self has crept into the church, robbing us of our eternal perspective. Yet it remains God's desire to fill our hearts to overflowing with an eternal great and glorious hope—and it's called "heaven."

In an effort to answer the main questions most believers have about heaven and to give us a place to hang our thoughts, I have divided this study as follows: We are going to look at the *rest*, the *relationships*, the *rewards*, and the *radiance* of heaven.

THE REST OF HEAVEN

By rest I mean the place where we lay our burdens down and come into that glorious place of peace. On earth, we have a great need for rest. It is God Himself who invented the Sabbath day, the taking of one day off a week. He instructed His people to take a day off and rest. It is needful after a long season of labor.

Once, a group from our church went to Japan and China. Before we left, I was very tired. We had started the church about nineteen months earlier and there are many things that go into starting a new church in a new city. About this time, it was catching up with me and I was tired. In addition, I had just finished teaching a series on spiritual warfare, and any time you teach on spiritual warfare or the devil or sin, you are opening yourself up for more attacks than usual.

We went to Japan; we preached, we taught, and we traveled. Then we went to China to take in Bibles. By the end of the trip I was much more tired than I had been when I left.

When we came back, I told Cindy that I needed a rest. She said that she needed a rest, too; because, if you're married to a pastor, then you are in it with him. There is just no getting around that, and we are a team effort. I suggested that we leave for a week and go away to the closest thing we could find to paradise and do something different from what we had been doing for a while.

We packed our bags, went to the airport, and flew away to Hawaii to the island of Maui, making certain we would be back in time for the next Sunday service.

It was the closest thing we could find to paradise. Rather than doing nothing, we did just the things that we wanted to do. We made sure that the things we did didn't make us too tired because we were there to rest. We lay in the sun, swam in the ocean, ate our favorite foods, drove around sightseeing, and had a wonderful time of rest. I share that because it is important to point out that our rest consisted of doing things we really enjoyed, not just lying around doing nothing. As it often does, time went by too fast and we were back in the labor again; but this is the nature of our rest here on this earth.

We are going to a place where we are going to rest forever. Some people have the idea that when they get to heaven they are going to do nothing; they think that they are going to lie down and rest forever. But that's not the rest of heaven. Others assume that they will be sitting around on a cloud playing a harp, or standing around wearing a white robe with a nice gold belt. But the rest of heaven will not be lying around doing nothing; it will actually involve doing things that we really enjoy doing.

In Revelation 14:13 John writes, "Then I heard a voice from heaven saying to me, 'Write: Blessed are the dead who die in the Lord from now on.' 'Yes,' says the Spirit, 'that they may rest from their labors, and their works follow them.'" We are going to be resting while we are working.

Rudyard Kipling got close to the idea when he said, "When Earth's last picture is painted and the tubes are twisted and dried,/ When the oldest colours have faded, and the youngest critic has died,/ We shall rest, and, faith, we shall need it—lie down for an aeon or two,/ Till the Master of All Good Workmen shall put us to work anew."

God is going to give each one of us something to do forever that will somehow be related to what we have been doing for Him in this life. However, it will all be a blessing and rest even while we labor for Him because we will be free from the presence of sin.

Freedom from Sin

The heart of this issue of resting from our labors in heaven is *freedom from sin.* It is ceasing from our labor in sin. My own spiritual warfare has to do with my own sin—the sin that lies within me. We need rest for our flesh, rest from the devil, and rest from the sin. We are going to find a rest from all of these things in heaven.

Revelation 21:4 says, "And God will wipe away every tear from their eyes; there shall be no more death, nor sorrow, nor crying; and there shall be no more pain, for the former things have passed away." That is rest from the effects of sin. There is much anxiety and stress that comes from sin and from allowing it to wear us down.

Free from Satan

We find in Revelation 20:10 that we are going to cease from our labor in terms of our warfare with the devil. "And the devil, who deceived them, was cast into the lake of fire and brimstone where the beast and the false prophet are. And they will be tormented day and night forever and ever." The day is going to come when he is going to receive eternal torment.

140

New Bodies

1 Corinthians 15:42 deals with the fact that we are going to be released from the labor of this decaying body: "So also is the resurrection of the dead. The body is sown in corruption, it is raised in incorruption."

Paul the apostle summed it up best when he said, "O wretched man that I am! Who will deliver me from this body of death?" (Romans 7:24). In heaven we will have glorified bodies which will never get tired, sick, or old.

The rest of heaven is from our decaying, corruptible bodies. It is rest from our warfare with the devil and a rest from the sin that lies within us. What a glorious day that will be! Yet, as if all this wouldn't be heaven enough in itself, the Lord has even more changes awaiting us.

THE RELATIONSHIPS OF HEAVEN

"What kinds of relationships are we going to have in heaven?" We will have an ongoing relationship with the angels. We are told in the Word of God that we are going to surround God's throne and worship with the angels forever, and that we are going to be served by angels in heaven. Hebrews 1:14 asks us, "Are they not all ministering spirits sent forth to minister for those who will inherit salvation?" Angels are the servants of the redeemed. We are told in 1 Corinthians 6:3, "Do you not know that we shall judge angels? How much more, things that pertain to this life?" Somehow we are going to rule over angels and they are going to serve us, and yet we will have a wonderful fellowship with them.

Will We Know Each Other?

One of the big questions that people ask is, "Will we know each other in heaven?" Perhaps the real question is, "Will we recognize ourselves?" The answer to this is "yes"—because we are going to be who we are forever. We are not going to be exactly like we are right now, but we will retain the personality, the essence, that uniqueness of who we are.

Genesis 25:8 says, "Then Abraham breathed his last and died in a good old age, an old man and full of years, and was gathered to his people." This verse implies that when Abraham died, he went to join all of his friends, people, and relatives.

In Matthew 8:11, Jesus gives a very clear statement about our identity in heaven. He says, "And I say to you that many will come from east and west, and sit down with Abraham, Isaac, and Jacob in the kingdom of heaven." Abraham is going to be Abraham, Isaac is going to be Isaac, and Jacob is going to be Jacob.

On the Mount of Transfiguration, God gave the disciples a glimpse of the glory of heaven. Jesus was talking with Moses and Elijah and somehow the disciples recognized them: "Then Peter answered and said to Jesus, 'Lord, it is good for us to be here; if You wish, let us make here three tabernacles: one for You, one for Moses, and one for Elijah'" (Matthew 17:3-4).

What about My Family?

"What about friends and family? Will I see them again?" Paul the apostle was addressing that very question in the book of 1 Thessalonians. He said, "But I do not want you to be ignorant, brethren, concerning those who have fallen asleep, lest you sorrow as others who have no hope."

They had a problem; some of their loved ones had died and gone to be with Jesus and they were wondering if they were ever going to see them again. "I do not want you to be ignorant or in sorrow. Do not be like the others who have no hope." And then he continues: "For if we believe that Jesus died and rose again, even so God will bring with Him those who sleep in Jesus.

For this we say to you by the word of the Lord, that we who are alive and remain until the coming of the Lord will by no means precede those who are asleep. For the Lord Himself will descend from heaven with a shout, with the voice of an archangel, and with the trumpet of God. And the dead in Christ will rise first. Then we who are alive and remain shall be caught up together with them in the clouds to meet the Lord in the air. And thus we shall always be with the Lord." He concludes with, "Therefore comfort one another with these words" (1 Thessalonians 4:13-18).

He tells them, "Do not be sad; do not be sorry; you are going to be reunited with your loved ones." God has it all worked out. Yes, we are going to be together.

What about My Spouse?

"What about my spouse? Will we still be married?" The answer comes in the Gospel of Matthew, where Jesus has an encounter with the Sadducees. They come to Jesus and tell Him about a hypothetical situation: "'Now there were seven brothers; the first one married and then he died and left his wife to his brother.... The next one married her, then the next one, and the next one... and finally the woman died also. Therefore, in the resurrection, whose wife of the seven will she be?...' And Jesus said to them, 'You are mistaken, not knowing the Scriptures nor the power of God. For in the resurrection they neither marry nor are given in marriage, but are like angels of God in heaven'" (Matthew 22:25-30).

Jesus says that there will be no marriages in heaven as we know them here on earth. If we go back to the beginning, we will see that one of the main reasons that man and woman came together to be married was because Adam needed help. The Bible says, "It is not good that man should be alone..." (Genesis 2:18). God said that he needed help. His actual words were, "I will make him a helper."

Eve needed a spouse because she needed protection. When she wandered off alone, she was deceived. The Bible says that Adam was not deceived. Because the woman needs protection, God brought her together with the man.

Why, then, do we not need marriage in heaven? First, in heaven we will all be perfect; we are not going to need help any more. Second, in heaven women will not need a protector any more; so, in that sense, you won't need to be married. Another reason God made marriage in the beginning was to produce children; therefore, a third reason is that there will be no children born in heaven because heaven will only be populated by the redeemed. Thus, there is no need for marriage in heaven because we will be perfect, with all of our needs perfectly met.

We are free to enjoy companionship together in heaven forever. If, after you get to heaven, you still want to be together, then you have that option. I want to get to know my wife, Cindy, much more in our perfect state.

Right now we are both still bound by our humanness, which sometimes creates problems between us. In that day we will both be perfect; hence, we will be able to enjoy unhindered fellowship in a way previously unknown to us.

In 1 Peter 3:7 it says, "Likewise you husbands, dwell with them with understanding, giving honor to the wife, as to the weaker vessel, and as being heirs together of the grace of life..."

This verse seems to indicate that for married couples there will be a mutual enjoyment of eternal life. That is an encouraging thought to me. Cindy and I have labored side by side here in the battle and we have seen the enemy come against our lives in so many ways. Therefore, having known together many of the sorrows and imperfections of this life, we are planning on spending a lot of time rejoicing together in the incorruptible glory of heaven.

What about Our Children?

Now about children. Many people may have had the tragedy of losing a child. And the question comes up, "What about the children who have died?" We can gain some insight into this question from an incident that occurred with David.

When David's little infant son died, David cast himself on the mercy of God and said, "But now he is dead; why should I fast? Can I bring him back again? I shall go to him, but he shall not return to me" (2 Samuel 12:23). Little children and babies who have died have gone to be with Jesus. Jesus took time to pick up the little children and hold them tenderly. He said to allow little children to come to Him (Matthew 19:14). Those who have died already are with Jesus and we are going to see them there.

These are the relationships of heaven. Isn't it wonderful to know that we will have relationships with angels, old friends, spouses, and the children? No wonder David said he wanted to dwell there forever!

A. A. Hodge put it so well when he wrote these words: "Heaven, as the eternal home of the divine Man and of all the redeemed members of the human race, must necessarily be thoroughly human in its structure, conditions, and activities. Its joys and its occupations must be rational, moral, emotional, voluntary, and active. There must be the exercise of all faculties, the gratification of all tastes, the development of all talent capacities, and the realization of all ideals. The reason, the intellectual curiosity, the imagination, the aesthetic instincts, the holy affections, the social affinities, and the inexhaustible resources of strength and power native to the human soul must all find in heaven exercise and satisfaction" (A. A. Hodge, *Evangelical Theology*, Carlisle, Penn.: Banner of Truth Trust, 1976, p. 400).

God intends that we will come to the day when we will be fully satisfied in all of those areas. Those are the relationships of heaven.

REWARDS OF HEAVEN

"What about the rewards in heaven?" It's hard to understand what rewards might be like in heaven. We have a lot of impressions which are based on the reward system we have here on earth.

It reminds me of the time when I was a young boy going to grammar school. Somebody announced that on the weekend there was going to be a track meet at the school. But only about three people showed up. We took off our shoes, the gun went off, and I ran like the wind down that grassy track. I hit the finish line, beating my opponent by about an inch. Only two people were in the stands cheering, but it was glorious to me. They handed me a little blue ribbon. That's the only blue ribbon I ever received in my life. I took it home, wearing it pinned on my chest, and then I hung it on the wall, showing it to all of my friends.

Then there was a city track meet, where all the runners in the last races were invited to participate. This time, the stands were filled with hundreds of people. I ran in that race with lots of boys, but I fell on the track. I picked myself up and cried all the way home. And when I got there, I threw that stupid ribbon away.

That's the kind of idea that we have when we think of rewards in heaven. We think of a little ribbon that we are going to tack onto ourselves. When I got beaten in that second track meet, the rest of the day was horrible and the day after was even worse. But in heaven there isn't going to be any day after when it comes to getting our rewards. We are going to get our rewards, and we are going to go on forever in the glory of having received them.

Our rewards in heaven are not going to be some little things we tack onto our shirts. They aren't going to be badges that God is going to give us that say, "Well done." Our rewards in heaven are going to have to do with our eternal life. One of our rewards will be taking part in *holy worship*. One of the greatest joys in life is to worship God, and this is our destiny.

Our worship is far less than perfect, but in heaven it's going to be absolutely perfect. I love to worship together with God's people, but there is the problem of distractions. Sometimes you are deep in worship when somebody next to you is talking about the ball game and you can hear them over your shoulder.

Some churches have the kind of freedom in their worship where their elders have felt led to tell the people to do whatever they want to do: kneel, stand up, anything they want to do, as long as it is done decently and in order. Those people are having a good time and they have prayed about that, but others will go to that church and wonder, "Why do they stand up whenever they feel like it? Why don't they wait until the worship leader says to stand?"

There isn't any church where everybody is going to love the way they do the worship. God, in His infinite goodness, has given us many different ways to worship Him.

The day is coming when we are all going to stand around the throne of God—multitudes and multitudes— and we are going to worship God in holy, reverential awe without distraction. We are all going to love the style because it's going to be God's perfect style.

The Bible says, "...and behold, a great multitude which no one could number, of all nations, tribes, peoples, and tongues, standing before the throne and before the Lamb, clothed with white robes, and with palm branches in their hands" (Revelation 7:9). Scripture says, "And I heard, as it were, the voice of a great multitude, as the sound of many waters and as the sound of mighty thunderings, saying,

147

'Alleluia! For the Lord God Omnipotent reigns!' " (Revelation 19:6).

Have you ever stood by a waterfall and heard the loud roar? That is what the apostle John is speaking of here.

Another area of rewards is that we are going to receive *crowns*. The Bible talks about four different kinds of crowns.

Crown of Rejoicing

There is the crown of rejoicing. In 1 Thessalonians 2:19, Paul says, "For what is our hope, or joy, or crown of rejoicing? Is it not even you in the presence of our Lord Jesus Christ at His coming?" The crown of rejoicing is being able to see those people in heaven that you, in your faithfulness, helped send there; being able to see them in the glory of heaven and knowing that they are there because you shared Jesus with them. That is the crown of rejoicing.

Daniel 12:3 says, "Those who are wise shall shine like the brightness of the firmament, and those who turn many to righteousness like the stars forever and ever." The crown of rejoicing is the joy that's going to flood our hearts forever, knowing that God used us to liberate these people out of sin. Daniel tells us that we are literally going to glow with that joy. That's the crown of rejoicing.

Crown of Righteousness

There is also a crown of righteousness. Paul tells us in 2 Timothy 4:8, "Finally, there is laid up for me the crown of righteousness, which the Lord, the righteous Judge, will give to me on that Day, and not to me only but also to all who have loved His appearing."

The crown of righteousness is the bliss of an eternally righteous existence that is completely void of any kind of sin to ruin it.

Crown of Life

We are told about the crown of life in James 1:12, "Blessed is the man who endures temptation; for when he has been proved, he will receive the crown of life which the Lord has promised to those who love Him." We will receive the crown of life for enduring temptations. To live forever with Jesus would be heaven enough for me.

Incorruptible Crown

Then, there is an incorruptible crown. Paul says, "And every man who strives for the mastery is temperate in all things. Now they do it to obtain a corruptible crown; but we [are going for] an incorruptible [crown]" (1 Corinthians 9:25, King James Version). As we are eternally enjoying the bliss of heaven, there isn't going to be anything that's going to be able to break through and destroy that. What God is giving us in heaven is absolutely incorruptible; nothing can ruin it or take it away.

Those are the four crowns. They are not little things you wear on your head; they are the essence of what life in heaven is all about.

Another reward is in an entirely different area—different from holy worship and the crowns. It is the idea of *glorified service*. Those other things are part of heaven; but the thing that is going to bring us great satisfaction forever is our glorified service. The thing that gives me the greatest joy is serving Jesus.

As we talk about glorified service, we are dealing with the issue of our position in heaven forever. You are going to have a position in heaven. We are told that we will cease from our labors, but that our labors will follow us. This means that we are going to be doing something.

In Matthew 25 we have the parable of the talents. Jesus tells about a King who goes away and gives out

149

these talents. This is a picture of Gospel privilege and spiritual gifts. Then He comes back for the day of accounting: "After a long time the lord of those servants came and settled accounts with them" (Matthew 25:19). This is the issue of accountability. God has given to each one of us a Gospel privilege and the primary responsibility *we* have with that is to give our lives to Christ. If you fail to do this, God cannot possibly allow you to enter into His heaven.

Second, because of the talents which God gives us, He will require those gifts of us. The Bible says, "...to whom much is given, from him much will be required..." (Luke 12:48). A great misconception is that we are not accountable. We, as Christians, will one day stand before God and give account for our faithfulness. We discover from the parable of the talents that after the day of accounting, He begins to hand out the rewards. He takes the person with five talents who says, "I have gained five more," and then He says to him, "You good and faithful servant; you have been faithful in a few things, I want to make you ruler over many things." The day of accounting is going to determine your position in heaven forever.

Individual

Beyond the issue of being accountable is the issue of being an individual. The Bible says, "he gave them talents; one received five, one received two, another received one." This represents your individual portion from God. He isn't concerned about how your neighbor did it; He's not concerned about how the other person did it; He's only concerned with what He has given you. You will be rewarded for what you have done with your individual portion, and that will give you your individual place of service forever. Just as you now have a unique place in the body of Christ, you will have a unique place in heaven and a function forever. We are not going to be lined up in white robes, sitting on our individual clouds, playing individual harps. We have a place, and it's going to be real. And it will be individual.

Relational

It will also be relational. What you do in heaven will be related to what you do here. Jesus says, "You've been faithful in a few things, I want to give you many things." Our deepest sense of reward in heaven will be our privilege of service.

THE RADIANCE OF HEAVEN

One last issue is "the radiance of heaven." That is all bound up in the New Jerusalem. The Bible says that God is going to make a new heaven and a new earth where there will be no sin. It will go on forever and the capital city is going to be a place called "New Jerusalem." God's glory is going to be there because God is going to dwell in the midst of His people in this New Jerusalem. Jesus says, "In My Father's house are many mansions... I go and prepare a place for you" (John 14:2-3). Your mansion is a dwelling place in the Father's house, and the Father's house is the New Jerusalem. That's where we are going to live; and that's where the glory is going to be focused. It will radiate from God's throne.

The Glory of the City

"The little girl was happily humming a hymn as she dusted the furniture to help her mother. 'Mommie, will I be dusting God's chair when I get to heaven, the way the hymn says?' she asked. Mother looked up with surprise. 'Which hymn, Honey?' 'And dust around the throne,' her little girl quoted. It took a while before the mother learned that she was quoting a line from the hymn 'Marching to Zion' with the phrase 'and thus surround the throne.'"

We will be there at His throne in the New Jerusalem, and we will see the glory of God there. There is going to be a rainbow over His throne and a river of life that bursts forth out of His throne going throughout all of New Jerusalem. John describes it as a bride adorned for her husband coming down out of heaven. He describes the entire city as being "transparent pure gold"; that means it's a glowing, bright place. He describes the foundation of the city as being like "bright jewels" and the gates as "pearls." The whole thing is made of transparent gold. That is our dwelling place forever, and we will be there with all of the redeemed of all of the ages.

In the midst of this wonderful city of radiant glory, God has planned to have a pure river of the water of life that we can drink from. In the middle of the street on either side, there is the tree of life. On each tree are twelve different kinds of fruit which they bear every month; and the leaves are for the healing of the nations.

The Size of the City

We are told that John watched as an angel measured the city. According to Revelation 21:16, the New Jerusalem is fifteen hundred miles long, fifteen hundred miles wide, and fifteen hundred miles high. It actually contains 2.25 million square miles. It is amazing if you compare it to the City of London, which contains an area of only one square mile and has a population of five thousand. On that basis, the New Jerusalem would be able to house more than one hundred billion people! Jesus said, "I am going to prepare a place for you." And He's been working on it for nearly two thousand years.

The New Jerusalem is large enough for the few who find the narrow way, but it won't confine them. This cube actually has the dimensions of the distance from Maine to Florida. It apparently has multiple levels and millions of intersecting golden avenues. It is a place of incredible majesty and beauty.

Harry Woods

Consider the following story of Harry Woods, recorded by Bethan Lloyd-Jones, the wife of the late D. Martyn Lloyd-Jones (affectionately known as the "Doctor").

She said: "We always had a prayer meeting on Good Friday morning, and I remember one especially. It was uplifting and quite outstanding. No one seemed to notice the time, and no one seemed to want the meeting to come to an end. Doctor stood at the door shaking hands as the people left. Harry Woods came along, and as he shook hands he said: 'Doctor, I am going home a very disappointed man.' Doctor could hardly believe his ears. 'Why do that?' he said, 'Didn't you enjoy the meeting? Didn't you?' But Woods broke across with these words, 'Doctor, I wanted to go straight to Heaven from the meeting, but it wasn't to be, and now I am just going home—I can't help feeling disappointed.'

"A year or more after this, we were in our regular Monday night prayer meeting and Doctor asked Harry Woods to open the meeting. The Word came alive as he read, and then he prayed. He seemed to lead us to the very gates of Heaven and a kind of awe fell upon us, when Harry began to sit down. As we bowed our heads again for the prayers of others, we heard a strange, whistling breathing. It got louder and louder and then stopped. We raised our heads to see two strong men catch Harry as he fell. They carried him out to the vestry. Doctor followed them as we sat, frozen in our seats.

"When he came back he told us that Harry Woods had gone to his eternal home in Glory. None of us was surprised; he had seemed to be there already as he prayed.

"Doctor prayed with us and we all went home sobered, amazed and thanking God for all we had seen and heard and felt" (Bethan Lloyd-Jones, *Memories of Sandfields*, Carlisle, Penn.: Banner of Truth Trust, 1983, pp. 16-17).

Harry Woods was a man who was full of the hope of heaven. One day he went there. One of these days, those of us who know Jesus and have followed Him as our Good Shepherd are going there, too. We are going to dwell forever in that glory of God Himself, and He's going to wipe away every tear and every bit of pain, and we will behold the face of the Lamb of God for all of eternity. This is the hope of every child of God who has come out of the darkness to follow Jesus in the kingdom of His light and life.

Heaven

This book was based on a series of messages that have been combined into an 8 tape cassette album on "Psalm 23". For further information on this series and other books or tapes by Danny Bond call (714)770-7650 or write:

The Word Transfer/Pacific Hills Church
PO Box 30730
Laguna Hills, CA 92654

New number 1-800-852-2229